Don't Read This Book!

Jim Auer

Liguori
ONE LIGUORI DRIVE
LIGUORI MO 63057-9999
314.464.2500

To all my wonderful teachers...
especially my wife, my children,
and my students.

. . . .

Imprimi Potest:
James Shea, C.SS.R.
Provincial, St. Louis Province
The Redemptorists

Imprimatur:
+ Paul A. Zipfel, V.G.
Auxiliary Bishop, Archdiocese of St. Louis

ISBN 0-89243-908-4
Library of Congress Catalog Card Number: 96-75300

This book is a revised and updated edition of *What's Right? A Teenager's Guide to Christian Living,* © 1987, Liguori Publications.

Scripture quotations are taken from the *New Revised Standard Version Bible,* copyright © 1989 by the Division of Christian Education of the National Council of the Churches of Christ in the U.S.A. Used by permission. All rights reserved.

Cover design by Chris Sharp

Contents

1. Not an Introduction   1

2. $2.4 Million…$7.9 Million… (Your Personal Worth)   4

3. The Really Big Why   7

4. Filters (Neither Coffee nor Oil)   10

5. Cave People and Wrapping Paper   14

6. Dismissed for Lack of Evidence   17

7. Does God Need a Makeover?   20

8. ?????????????? (And Maybe ? Too!)   23

9. Who's Talking to Whom?   26

10. Pig, Duck, or Cow: Does It Depend?   29

11. Life Preservers   33

12. The S-Word: It's Not a Loch Ness Monster   37

13. Morality Is Not Just a Weird Apple Pie   41

14. You're Responsible for Your Beeper   44

15. So Many Voices   47

16. Fony Phreedom   52

17. You Only Live (and Die, Too) Once   56

18. Sex (No Need for Fancy Titles Here)   59

19. Sex II   63

20. Sex III: The !#ld%!m*n Crocodiles   68

21. Previews and Underwear   71

22. Metamorphosis!! ("Look It Up.")   75

23. 2 Minus 1 and Other Differences   79

24. Rational Ice for Seventh-Commandment Pain   82

25. To Beat or Not to Beat the System   86

26. Club Membership   90

27. Getting Sucked into the War Machine   93

28. UFOs and Seven-Year-Old Warriors   97

29. Yes, You're One of *Them!*   100

30. Some Final Stuff   104

. . . .

CHAPTER ONE

Not an Introduction

"**M**r. Jenkins, this question wasn't in the book."

"I know. The answer was, though."

"Mr. Jenkins, I'm serious. Right here—number 4. I skimmed back over every chapter, and I'm positive there wasn't anything on this."

"You're right."

"Well, then, how can you..."

"The answer was in the introduction."

"Aw, come on—we had to read the INTRODUCTION?"

Author: You're reading this book.

Reader: No kidding—you could tell, huh?

Author: Yeah. It's the way you have the book in front of you and your eyes are going across the words on the page. Sort of gives it away. Old trick I picked up.

Reader: So what's your point?

Author: I'm wondering why. Why are you reading this book?

Reader: I could stop if that's what you want. In fact...

Author: No, please don't. This is only chapter 1. We've hardly met. I'm just interested in your reason. You could be doing something else.

Reader: Well, depending on who I am, the reasons could be pretty different. Like, maybe I'm a natural-born seeker of truth and similar things like the meaning of existence, see, and also I need a structure to mold my life around, and your book looks like it has all that and lots more.

Author: Excuse me, but you mentioned *truth*.

Reader: The book looked a *little* interesting.

Author: That's better. And thanks. Other reasons?

Reader: Do your feelings get hurt easily?

Author: I got upset once when this girl I was dating said I was a terrible dancer. But she married me anyway, so I got over it. Besides, she was right. Go ahead; I can handle the truth.

Reader: Well, depending on the situation, there's a chance that somebody is *making* me read it—like, if it's part of a class or a religious-education thing. Or *strongly expecting* me to read it. You know, like maybe I got it as a gift for some occasion and...

Author: Instead of a new CD or a Porsche?

Reader: Yeah, and they'll be asking me questions about it.

Author: Some people are like that.

Reader: My turn. Why did you *write* it?

Author: I didn't really intend to. I was on my way to play racquetball instead, but when they offered me thousands upon thousands of...

Reader: Excuse me, but you mentioned *truth*.

Author: Right. Well, the truth is, I like talking to young people. My wife and I have two of our own. They're in their twenties now.

Reader: What are their names?

Author: Jeff and Jeannie. My wife's name is Rose.

Reader: What's *your* name?

Author: Jim. But listen, you should get in the habit of noticing the author's name. Some teachers—this is true—ask trick questions like "Who was the author of the book?" Anyway, besides our own two kids, I've taught somewhere around three thousand others. Some of them are really old now. They're even in their *thirties*.

From teaching them, I picked up a few things. I learned that those who really try to find out and do what's right and what's real have ended up happier. A lot happier. So I thought I'd talk about that.

Reader: Are you going to lecture and be boring?

Author: Me? Lecture? You kids these days! You think you know it all, but let me tell you a thing or two about...

Reader: Stop.

Author: ...five miles every day through the ice and snow to school...

Reader: STOP! You *are* joking, right?

Author: Yeah.

Reader: Thank God.

Author: Good idea. We'll get to that fairly shortly. Almost right away, in fact. Want to get started? Actually, we already have. As of right now, we're almost finished with chapter 1.

Reader: Why didn't you call this the introduction?

Author: Trust me; there was a reason.

$2.4 Million...$7.9 Million...
(Your Personal Worth)

"I hear 1.3 million, 1.3 million is the bid, do I hear 1.5? We have 1.5 million, do I hear 1.8, 1.8 or better? Yes, there it is, we have 1.8 million, 1.8 million for the sense of hearing, we're looking for, we have 2.3 million from the lady in the blue dress, 2.3 million is the current bid, do I hear 2.6 million? 2.6 million from the gentleman in the far corner, 2.6 million for hearing, worth far more, of course, do we have we have 3 million? 3 million from the lady in the orange and brown floral, 3 million for the sense of hearing, 3 million and still open, do I hear..."

—*A fantasy auction*

Some people are lucky enough to almost get killed without even getting hurt. For example, they step into a street without looking, and a huge truck grinds to a stop a couple of inches before it would have flattened them into something resembling those Saturday-morning cartoon characters that are always getting flattened by big rocks. Except that they wouldn't have recovered and resumed their normal shape a few seconds later. Maybe the front of the truck even nudges them a tiny bit right before it comes to a complete halt.

Why is this a lucky experience? Because one of the best ways to appreciate something is to have it taken away, or (as in this case) very vividly *almost* taken away. An experience like this would dramatically refresh your awareness of the most basic and wonderful gift we have: *life.*

Because life is as basic as, well, life can get, we don't think about it much. It's probably been a while since the last time you heard the alarm clock, sat up in bed, and thought, "Hey, this is terrific—I'm alive again today!" If you'd had a near encounter with a truck, that might be your regular mode of beginning each day, at least for quite some time. You'd be grateful just for *being*.

The same is true of your non-liquid life worth—which will take a little explanation.

There have been times when I've had under five bucks in my billfold and not much more than that in my checking account. And occasions when I've felt worth less than that because of the amounts in my billfold and checking account. That's because I was (a) using messed up thinking, and (b) even in money terms, thinking only of liquid cash.

Liquid cash is a term that finance people use. It's one of the few terms they use that I actually understand. (Put me in charge of Wall Street, and the national economy will look like a sandcastle after a tidal wave.) Liquid cash means dollars you can actually spend.

It's not the same as *worth*, even financial worth. Let's say somebody gives you a mint-condition '66 Mustang or that brand new Porsche we mentioned in the first chapter. You can't spend them at a department store, but they're worth a lot, and you can enjoy owning and using them. They're part of your (in this case) financial worth.

As a person, you have worth that can't possibly be measured in financial terms, but we can give it a shot anyway, to make a point.

Let's say medical science has advanced to the point that sensory-organ implants are expensive but quite routine and successful as long as the body chemistry between organ donor and receiver are a good match. And let's say that a *very* wealthy person is in need of hearing. After a nationwide search, it's determined that your body chemistry matches perfectly. He or she is offering a million dollars for your hearing.

One…million…dollars. And this kind of transaction is tax exempt, by the way, so it's a pure one-million-dollar profit. Think of the places you could go, although you wouldn't be able to hear any of the people or the music or anything else going on there. Is it a deal?

Probably not. Okay, same situation, only now the wealthy person needs your eyesight. The offer is two million, and you can probably up it to two and a half or so. Think of what you could buy; you just wouldn't see any of it. And, of course, you'd have to give up driving and things like that. Is it a deal for $2.5 million?

Probably not. How about five million—no, let's make it *ten* million in exchange for your ability to move? You'd be a millionaire ten times over, but you'd be permanently paralyzed. Deal?

How about ten million—no, let's make it ten *billion* for your consciousness? All your mental abilities and awareness. You'd be a ten-billionaire, except that you wouldn't know it because you'd be in a permanent coma. Deal?

Dumb question.

And we haven't even hit the big stuff yet.

Like the fact that you're not scheduled to see, hear, move, talk, think, and make decisions only for a few decades and then that's it, that's the end of you. The network's still in business, but your show's been canceled.

You're headed toward forever, which is a *really* long time. But from the previews God has given us, it's not the kind of slow, dragging forever that a Friday-afternoon class in a hot schoolroom feels like. Unless you completely screw the plan up by the way you live, it's a breathtakingly exciting, joy-filled forever so spectacular we can't begin to imagine it.

Try a wild experiment. Actually, it's not wild at all; it only seems that way because we seldom do it even though we should. Go alone somewhere, relax, and take ten slow, deep breaths, being aware of each one. And then tell God thanks. Actually say it.

Take ten steps, being conscious of your legs moving. Say thanks again. Pick out an object—a vase, a flower, a computer, a mixer-blender, anything—and study its shape and color and texture. Tune in to whatever sounds are around you; see how many different ones you can pick up.

And once more, say thanks for your "non-liquid life worth." You've just enjoyed part of your multi-maxi-mega-trillion dollar account in the bank of human life and nature, without using any of it up. It's all still there.

And really worth saying thanks for.

CHAPTER THREE

The Really Big Why

"Well, here we are. You've arrived at the final step. This is it."

"I can't believe it. I still can't believe it."

"Now remember, audience, please, we need absolute quiet. A correct answer to this final question will win our already very successful contestant five new cars, trips to Hawaii, Tahiti, London, and Paris, a heart-shaped swimming pool, a fluorescent orange grand piano, forty million dollars, twenty-five pounds of designer paper clips, and a ten-year supply of cream rinse and dog food. Are you ready?"

"I'm ready, Pat."

I couldn't be on a game show, even though I occasionally remember trivia like which long-dead nations signed the Treaty of Whatever—which is not nearly as valuable as remembering where I put the car keys.

In case I blew every question, I'm not a good enough actor to be like those people who don't upset the champion, those who sometimes walk away with absolute zero showing on their monitors. "Well, Jack," the host says, "you came up blank, but we've really enjoyed having you on the show. We've got some nice consolation prizes backstage for you to take home before you leave."

Jack smiles and acts like finally getting on the show after years of trying and then coming away with nothing was the most fun he's had since he was ten years old and went hunting for worms in his backyard. I give people like him a lot of credit. I'm not sure I'd cover disappointment that well.

But let's fantasize about you, not me. You've made it onto a game show, you've been the current champion for weeks, and now it's time for you to exit with a chance for unbelievable prizes. You'll be asked one, final Ultimate Question. A correct answer will bring you almost everything but the continent of North America in prizes. It'll be a very special question, obviously. Not one of the usual "who, what, when, where" questions. This one is a "why" question.

Why are you here on earth?

Okay, that's not a likely game-show question, even for the biggest prize ever. But it's a great question. Worth spending some time on now and then.

Why *are* you here on earth?

It invites lots of cute answers like "Well, because one night, see, my mom and dad, uh...." That covers cause and effect and biology, but it's really weak on *purpose,* which is what we're after here.

Things like "to give that cute exchange student a reason to stay in this country" plug into the idea of purpose, and even get interesting, but you can tell they're not the ultimate bottom line.

Back when the original game shows were really big on prime-time television, contestants were sometimes allowed to have a guest expert help them answer the top-level questions. Maybe you should bring in a guest expert.

A carpenter from Nazareth, perhaps.

This carpenter from Nazareth, who was also the Son of God and our Savior, put it like this: Love the Lord your God...love your neighbor as yourself.

You were put here by God who *is* love to channel and spread the love that you came from and help it grow.

The answer's that simple?

Yes.

Trouble is, simple doesn't mean easy. Living out that answer day after day is definitely not easy. For one thing, lots of stuff goes around advertised as love when it's not. Anything from cheap sex to covering for a friend who's into a destructive, alcohol- or marijuana-filled lifestyle.

Love means doing what is really, genuinely good for yourself and for other people.

Sometimes that gives you a wonderful warm glow or even puts you on a great emotional high. You find a crying three-year-old in the mall, give him or her a hug, dry the tears, pick up the dropped teddy bear, and reunite him or her with mommy...what a great feeling. Nothing wrong with enjoying it, either.

But sometimes loving means doing things that are difficult, things that don't get noticed, things you're not crazy about, that even the person you love isn't crazy about and doesn't appreciate at the time. (Sometimes people whom you're trying to help act like a dog that's about to chomp into a glob of poisoned ground beef thrown by a cranky neighbor. You know what it is; Spot doesn't. Spot might even get a little nasty when you try to separate him from the ground beef. You do it out of love anyway.)

This isn't putting God out of the picture, incidentally. We very much need a one-on-one relationship and frequent conversation with God, or we'll bypass a lot of those chances to channel and spread the love we came from. But in much of our daily lives, in sheer hours out of the day, God chooses to relate with us through other people. "Do you see a human being around anywhere? That's me. Do something good."

On a game show, winning the big prize is really just the start. How you spend or use it is the real payoff.

Same way with life. Knowing that we're on earth to accept, channel, and spread God's love is just the start. Then comes doing it. It could be something really spectacular; it could be something so ordinary most people would miss it.

That fits the illustrations of loving others that Jesus mentioned. One was laying down one's life for another. The other was giving someone a drink of water.

· · · · · · · · · ·

CHAPTER FOUR

Filters (Neither Coffee nor Oil)

"For me...I guess it's basically...a playground. Yeah, I think that's it. A playground. Or an amusement park. A big party room. That kind of place."

"Pretty much like a prison. Sometimes more like a concentration camp."

"A boxing ring. Or maybe a wrestling ring. Someplace where you stomp on the other guy, you know?"

"An outhouse. It's obvious. All you have to do is look around you. It's a toilet."

"An island. My own island, all mine. And usually just me there."

"Just this big, dull room, not much in it. That's about all, the way I see it. A big, dull room."

"A courtroom. I'm usually guilty."

"A road to success. You floor the gas pedal, go for your goals, and pick up cool stuff along the way."

—*A few filters*

I had a blind friend who saw life better than most people with sight. But then he had a wonderful filter. It was clear, with very few distortions, and put things in the right perspective. A great filter. I often wished mine were that good.

Here's an example of how this kind of filter works. Three cars pull up at an intersection and stop for a traffic light. On the corner is a group of teenagers. They're just hanging out. There's a sudden burst of laughter in the group.

The first driver thinks, "That's neat—kids having fun, enjoying life. Youth is a great thing. Sometimes I wish it lasted longer."

Second driver thinks, "Wonder what kind of filthy joke somebody just told. Or maybe they just figured out how they're going to get their hands on some beer so they can get drunk later on."

Third driver thinks, "They're laughing at me. I guess I look pretty strange to them. Maybe I *am* strange. Maybe I *am* out of touch with real life."

Different filters.

Everybody has one. Call it the way you look at life. Actually, everybody has several filters. We switch them from time to time, depending on what's been happening in our lives, and sometimes we automatically switch from one to another depending on what we're looking at. But usually one of them is what we look through most of the time.

Some people's filters are so twisted that what comes through isn't remotely like what's out there at all. People who see alien invaders among a crowd of perfectly normal people and UFO landing marks among the oil streaks in a parking lot have filters like that.

The quotations at the beginning of this chapter illustrate a few common filters, ways of *usually* seeing life. "Usually" is important. Even the person who sees life as a big, dull room will once in a while experience something as fun and will say so.

What's your usual way of looking at life? Thinking about it is more than an amusing little exercise in psychology. How you view yourself and your world will have a lot to do with how you think and feel about God. And we have a way of coming up with images of God (based on the filter we're using) that God probably looks at and says, "My Self! That's not Me at all!"

Take the person who sees life as a courtroom and himself or herself as the defendant...who's nearly always guilty. How would someone arrive at a view like this? There are many causes and explanations, but right now we're concerned with the results.

For example, it's going to be difficult for this person to see or at least to feel God as a loving parent. God may seem to loom over him or her as a stern, sentencing judge. Or perhaps God will seem like a let-down, even disgusted parent who's thinking, "I'm *really* disappointed in you. You *could* have turned out so well; you *could* be so good...but you never are. It's a shame. Makes me think maybe I should have put my plans and efforts into someone else, someone different."

And if *that's* how you think someone feels about you, it pretty well poisons and paralyzes your hope and enthusiasm for deepening a relationship with that person.

What about seeing life as a road to success and yourself as a born-to-win achiever? Life would be more fun for a person who sees it that way, and it would probably bring about a more positive view of God. Most people find it easier to feel the warmth of God's love when things are going well in their lives.

But it could also push God into an outsider's role in that person's life, especially if he or she is a very talented person for whom success and achievement come frequently and *apparently* (remember: *apparently*) without much input or help from God. God then appears to be like a grandparent who sits in a rocker on a far corner of the porch and smiles...but doesn't have much advice or help for living in the fast-lane, real world.

The world is a playground, or ought to be, or you try to make it be? That filter might help you see God as a provider of joy and excitement. It could also lead you to see God as a playground supervisor who (a) would never think of actually taking part in the games, or (b) isn't being very good at his job during those times when life isn't much fun.

How do *you* look at life? What's your usual filter? It's worth spending some time on. You'll come out with a better understanding of yourself, and a better understanding of how you see God and why you see God that way.

Through all of this, of course, God *is* who God *is*.

Which is...?

You ought to check into it. As an old cereal commercial used to say, "It's the right thing to do." It may take a little time. Maybe a lifetime. Which doesn't mean you can wait till you're seventy to start.

You can start by walking mentally up to God and asking. It doesn't have to be fancy. "Who are you and what are you like?" will do fine, and you might even add, "I'd like some help identifying my filter and how it affects how I see you."

Ask a bunch of times. God likes to be bugged. Keep at it, and sooner or later you're going to come up with an answer. When you do, tell yourself. That's the person who needs to know.

CHAPTER FIVE

· · · · · · · · ·

Cave People and Wrapping Paper

"Oh my gosh, I wonder what this is! Who wrapped this? Did you wrap this, Carl? It's so pretty I hate to take the paper off. I'll be careful and save the bow. There. Okay, here goes...oh my gosh, would you look at this IT'S A BOX! Oh, it's just GORGEOUS! Look it's got a top and a bottom and four sides! I'll bet it's genuine cardboard, too. Is it, Carl? It IS? I thought so! And look how it has all that SPACE inside! It's just perfect."

Cave people were religious. Probably pretty hairy and blunt of manners, but definitely religious.

How do we know that? It's all over the insides of their caves. They didn't leave behind many hymnals, but they drew their understanding of God or gods quite a bit. It was obviously on their minds a lot.

Okay, that understanding of God is...well, we might call it pretty messed up by our standards, but we can't be smug and superior about that. We have the Word-of-God-in-flesh-and-bone-Jesus and the Word-of-God-in-inspired-writings-of-the-Bible to work with. That's like being given a sixty-billion-mile head start on arriving at the truth about what we call "religion."

But in one way, maybe they had a head start on us. A head start we might call "the gut reflection." They looked around outside themselves and looked around inside themselves and drew some conclusions. That's where religion begins.

Religion begins with knowing that you didn't start yourself (even pointing to your parents doesn't help much because they didn't start themselves either), that you don't have the power to keep yourself going forever, and that in the meantime you can't always survive or make sense of stuff by yourself.

Even on days when you feel like you're absolutely flying, able to conquer anything, you know that it doesn't explain the universe and probably won't last. Take a day when you score a B- on the nearly impossible physics midterm and celebrate by buying two new CDs and a large pizza with extra everything. Even then you know that you'll eventually forget the grade, that the groups who made the CDs may not be together a few years from now, and that the pizza won't make it past thirty minutes.

Religion begins with looking around at the whole world, everything from far-off galaxies to the stuff under your microscope slide, and realizing, "All this didn't just start itself. Couldn't have. Somebody made this." And then you realize that this Somebody must still be standing behind the scenes of this trillion-act life drama called Daily Life in the Universe.

That Somebody is called God.

Realizing that you are God's creation, that God must care about you, and that you need to respond to God and learn to act as you should…that's religion. At least that's where it begins. Without that beginning, it's kind of like this:

It's your birthday, okay, and you're not expecting the world and all its treasures, but…well, it's your birthday. In the morning you come down from your room and on the table is a nicely wrapped package with your name on the tag. It's from someone you might expect a present from.

You pick up the box. It feels pretty light, but that adds to the mystery. You shake it, but nothing rattles or rustles, so the mystery deepens. You break the ribbon, rip off the wrapping paper, open the package, and it's…empty. Except for a little piece of paper at the bottom that says, "Happy Birthday," signed by the person who sent the package. Well, sort of signed. Actually, the signature was put on with a rubber stamp. That's it.

Did you get a birthday *package?* Sure. Did you get a birthday *present?* Dumb question.

It didn't have to be colossal. Just something. Even something really small and inexpensive with a sincere note saying, "I'm sorry this is really all I can come up with right now." You wouldn't fault someone for honesty like that.

Religion is like that. Something has to be inside, no matter how pretty and "right" the outside looks. Something has to be inside for there to be a relationship with God.

We can say all the right things in front of other people: "Sure-I believe-in-God-he-made-everything-and-Jesus-he-died-on-the-cross-for-us-so-we-can-get-to-heaven-that's-really-cool-forever-and-ever-Amen." But we can have all the right answers and still be like that birthday package, the birthday-looking box that was empty on the inside.

The idea of filling up the inside scares us sometimes. Sometimes we're not certain what to put there, or we're not certain that God will like what we put there. Those are foolish fears, really. All we need to put on the inside of our relationship with God is us. Wherever we are on our journey with God, that's what God wants.

So what if we're still little kids spiritually? It's okay to be a little kid in some ways. Jesus himself said so.

About twenty years ago, my son brought me a piece of paper with a greeting scrawled in crayon: "dear dad thanks for being a good dad love jeff."

The letters were wobbly, the lines were uneven, and there was a terrible—no, actually a *wonderful*—lack of punctuation and capitalization. Did I read it and think, "This kid's writing style really needs some work"? Did I think, "I wish he were more grown up so he could write me something decent"? Not exactly. (If I *had*, I should have had my father's license revoked.)

I still have that piece of paper.

Bring God whoever you are and whatever you have inside you.

· · · · · · · · ·

CHAPTER SIX

Dismissed for Lack of Evidence

"Jason?"

"Oh, hi, Angela. What's up?"

"Jason...do you know what day this is?"

"Sure. It's Wednesday. 8:15 P.M."

"That's all? Anything else?"

"Sure. It's your birthday."

"We've been going together for two years and..."

"Happy birthday. Hope you're having a good one."

"JASON! I wasn't expecting rubies and diamonds, but it's my birthday! You didn't even give me a call!"

"Angela, baby, relax. I was just busy here watching a good video and playing cards with some friends, but I've been THINKING about you every now and then, and hoping you're having a nice birthday. Really, I've thought about it several times because...well, because you're really important to me, and I..."

"That's it? You THOUGHT about me?"

"Isn't it the thought that counts?"

Imagine you have a friend whose parents are always on his or her case to get good grades. They say it's so important. But when he or she *gets* good grades, the parents hardly notice. You were there once when your friend brought home a Student of the Quarter Award. You couldn't believe what you heard.

"Yes, that's nice, sweetie, now remember your father and I have that business dinner at the Hilton tonight, so you'll have to take your brother to...."

Imagine you have some friends who say they're really into sports. There's nothing like competition on the field or the court, they say, or at least watching great athletes on television.

But in spite of all the talk, they never play. They're not on any team in any sport. They don't shoot hoops on a playground. The sports equipment they own is stored away in closets. They don't even watch the Olympics, the World Series, the Super Bowl, or the NCAA or NBA finals on TV. But if you ask them what they think of sports, you'll hear, "Sports are life!"

All these people, including Angela's boyfriend, Jason, have something in common. Something that they *say* they have inside them just isn't showing up on the outside. It's the reverse of what we talked about in the last chapter.

This violates our sense of how things ought to be. We usually judge the intensity and the sincerity of people's ideas and feelings by *what they do about them.* Not just by how much they say, but by what they do.

It doesn't mean they have to succeed wildly at what they do. It's how often and sincerely they try. If someone practices golf twice a week and enters a tournament fourteen times but never wins, you still know that person is serious about golf.

What about believing in a God who created us and has a plan for us, believing there's a life after death, and knowing there's such a thing as good and evil but not doing anything about it? That's no different.

God doesn't expect you to have your mind on heavenly matters half the day. God doesn't expect you to get as wired and thrilled over reading the book of Exodus as you do over a game-winning goal or an invitation to the prom from the person of your dreams.

But our faith has to have an outside expression of what we believe on the inside. That's the way human nature operates. If something matters to us, it shows up in how we behave, in what we do.

This inside-outside aspect of human nature is so closely connected that if you stop doing something on the outside, *you tend to lose the part that used to be inside*. If a close friend moves far away and you can no longer share music and movies, pizza and problems and conversation, for a while there's a big empty spot. It may even seem as if you're closer than ever because you miss the other person so much.

But after some time passes, it's difficult to have the same intense feelings you formerly had for that person. It doesn't mean that love has turned to hate or even to total indifference. It's just that ideas and feelings and beliefs that aren't expressed tend to fade.

"My religion is completely in my heart. I don't need to go to church or say prayers or keep rules or practices and stuff like that. I think about my religion, and that's all that matters. That's what counts."

Kind of reminds you of Angela's boyfriend, Jason.

. . . .

CHAPTER SEVEN

Does God Need a Makeover?

"You want to be a doctor, right, Sandi? Tell us about your classes at med school."

"That'll be hard. See, I cut most of the classes."

"You do?"

"Boring things! Just a bunch of facts about bones and blood and organs and stuff. You know what medical schools need to do? They need to put some excitement into the classes. I mean, it's the same old stuff: This is a leg bone, that's an arm bone—I think that one's called a humus...no, humerus...something like that. But we did that in junior high. That's what I mean—they never do anything really different."

"Amanda, you're in med school too, right? Are you bored by all the classes too?"

"Well...yes and no. I mean, some of it's routine facts and pieces of knowledge, no doubt about that. But when I think that the more I know about, let's say, a humerus, the better I can help people who have a broken one and help give them part of their life back, which is an example of what I want to do with my life...that makes it exciting."

Problem is, God's perfect. We're not. Not any of us. Including Father Smith at Saint Michael's and Reverend Thompson at Eastwood United Methodist and Rabbi Goldstein at Rosedale Beth Adam Synagogue.

As we'll no doubt find out upon our first face-to-face meeting, God is immensely exciting and breathtakingly thrilling beyond anything we've experienced, dreamed about, or hoped for.

But Mrs. Ellerbe who plays the organ at Our Lady of Hope may not crank out immensely exciting and breathtakingly thrilling hymns—at least by your standards. Mr. Evans, the volunteer youth minister at First Baptist, may think that a car wash followed by a hot dog grill-out is such a kick that young people would want to have one at least twice a month except in December and January.

You get the idea. Not every activity that celebrates God nor every person who represents God in some way is fascinating and electrifying.

And can't be. There's the point. These are limited human beings we're talking about here. Even the literal divine presence of Jesus in our Catholic worship, the Mass, can be dulled by a dull approach to it.

And at that point, many people (including adults, not just younger people) drop out because of this unrealistic expectation: Anything to do with God should be nonstop exciting, or at least extremely interesting. "Call me when you know how to thrill me; maybe I'll come back." But that's pretty self-centered and demanding when you think about it. It's like Sandi's approach to classes at medical school.

It's also a demand we don't make in other areas. If you go out for volleyball or football or drama, you don't expect and demand that every meeting, every practice, every rehearsal be a continuing series of thrills. A good portion of it is somewhere between routine and just plain dull.

When the coach yells, "Take five more!" players seldom let out a huge cheer and say, "All *right!* We get to run five more laps! This is great!" When the director says, "Let's run it *again,*" you don't always see faces beam and hear the cast rejoice, "Yes! We get to do this scene for the *eighth* time in a row!"

They hang in.

We do this all the time with nearly everything we're involved in. When a favorite singer or group comes out with a new CD that's really pretty blah, people don't say, "Well, that's it. Take every album he/she/they ever recorded and throw it out. None of it's worthwhile anymore." If last year's team went to the city finals but this year's team finishes fifth in the division, we don't walk away muttering, "This is the last game *I* ever come to." If we have loyalty to what we're part of, we hang in through the slow times.

It's no different with God and our faith. At least it shouldn't be.

Let's take a look at Amanda's reaction to the same med school classes that bore Sandi. They're the same courses, same information, same activities. What makes the difference?

Amanda is bringing herself to them. Plugging them into her dreams, her visions, her plans, her future. Expecting to find something to work with, looking for it, being open to it. That's a lot different than showing up with an attitude: "I'm here. Entertain me."

This doesn't mean that religious activities are *supposed* to be dull so that you can suffer through them to show God how loyal you are. I often think of a comment from Sister Thea Bowman, a marvelous, beautiful, intensely spiritual black nun who was a convert to the Catholic faith: "Where I came from, the preacher told the people that if you come to church to praise the Lord, you're also gonna have a good time!" There's wisdom there that we can learn from.

Our walk with the Lord, including all the "religion things" we do, is in some ways like other things we do. It begins to come alive when we understand what's going on and what's at stake, and bring our whole selves to it. It's not God who needs the makeover; it's more likely to be us.

. . . .

?????????????????
(And Maybe ? Too!)

"**Y**ou'll never get an answer if you don't ask the question."
"Now THAT is a seriously stupid question."
"Do you ALWAYS have to question EVERYTHING?"
"I'll be glad to answer any questions you may have."
"This is your brain on drugs. Any questions?"
"The key to life is asking the right questions."
"Don't ask questions, just DO!"
"Answer all questions in complete sentences."
"And so the REAL question is...."
—*You've probably heard some of these*

When professional soccer becomes a widely televised national sport, you might be watching Chris Gaines. He's a good way beyond just good. As I'm writing this, he's in his mid-teens, but I remember when he was two or three years old and lived next door. I'd be walking down the driveway to my car.

"Way-yuh you go-un, Unca Jim?"

"To the post office."

"Why?"

"I have to mail a manuscript."

"Why?"

"Because it's due in three days."

"Why?"

"Because that's when I said I'd have it finished."

"Why?"

It would go on until I produced a satisfying answer to "Why?" but Chris wasn't finished: "When you go-un be baa-yuck?" I tried to be friendly and patient even when I was in a hurry and the questions sounded so unnecessary. Someday I'll ask Chris if he remembers whether I was or not.

Adults seem to have a love-hate affair with questions from kids. Sometimes they invite questions, at other times they seem irritated by them. But that's not really strange behavior. Questions come in hundreds of varieties, with widely different emotional impacts.

"Can you show me how to change the oil in the car?" is not the same as "Who are you going to vote for and why?" And the latter is not the same as "Who *says* we have to go to Church? What if somebody just made that up?"

Adults handle this last situation in different ways, some much better than others, just as young people ask questions in different ways, some much better than others. When you ask questions about God, faith, religious obligations and practices, and moral rules and guidelines, especially with an edge in your voice that sounds like attitude—whether you mean it to be there or not—you're entering an area that's probably important and personal to the person you're asking.

He or she may have worked on these same questions for quite some time and made conclusions that feel absolutely beyond doubt...and may not fully remember how he or she struggled with them. There's more: These are questions that deal with life and eternity and making sure we end up happy. In other words, the big stuff. If the adult cares about you at all, he or she wants you to have the right answers about the big stuff. There's a lot more at stake than usual; in fact, there's everything at stake.

But you're not wrong or bad for questioning things that for others, probably older than you, are pretty well settled or even locked in granite. God can handle doubts and questions much better than other people sometimes do, including doubts and questions about God and God-related things.

Here are a few thoughts or guidelines about handling questions of faith. I hope you find them helpful.

- If an answer to a deep religious question doesn't come quickly, whether beamed directly into your mind or sent through another person, that's not a signal to give up or conclude that there probably is *no* answer. That's not a signal to decide that this whole faith thing is just opinion, and one's as good as another, and if you never get an answer that's okay because it doesn't make any real difference, and so on. (We don't operate this way in other areas, like medicine, for example!)

- If something doesn't make perfect sense at a certain time, that doesn't mean it's probably worthless in general. There was a time when Mr. Edison wasn't positive about how to make a light bulb, but we're all glad he didn't decide it was a really dumb idea and quit.

- You owe it to yourself (and God) to run a gut-honest sincerity check. It goes like this: *Am I really, sincerely having a hard time accepting and making honest sense out of this...or am I simply looking for an excuse to get out of a religious obligation or guideline?* That's a tough but necessary question to ask; the second item can look and feel a lot like the first if we want it to.

- You *don't* have to have a ton of questions and doubts, or any. It's not a law. It's not a necessary condition for being a normal teenager or young adult. It's not an expectation that you should let your peers put on you. ("You're sixteen years old, for crying out loud! You still think you need to go to church and keep all those rules? You must have some weirdo religious virus or something.") Being your own self means not acting like a mindless piece of Play-Doh that somebody else manipulates, including your peers.

Give God a chance to work with you. It's okay with God that your faith isn't finished and set like concrete. Growth in faith often begins with a question. Ask God for help. God is thrilled when people bring honest questions. It means they care about the answers.

CHAPTER 9

• • • • • • •

Who's Talking to Whom?

"Let's see...there should be no problem with .00208332 first thing in the morning, or sometime early. Then we can probably whip in a little around noon, say maybe .00069444. Late afternoon, well, that depends on soccer practice or meetings and stuff, but maybe .00138888 would work there. Okay, now we're into the evening, which will depend on—oh, heck, we can squeeze .00277776 out of the evening somewhere. Now let's double check: .00208332 plus .00069444 plus .00138888 plus .00277776...equals twenty-four, carry the two...hey, it works out. We can do this."

Let's see, those figures come to .0069444. Rounded up, that's .007, which is 7 over 1,000. If you had 1,000 parts of something, and you used 6.9444 of them, you'd have a little over 993 left. That's a lot left. You could spare .0069444 of something without getting into a severe crunch. Let's keep those figures in mind just in case we need them. You never know.

In the meantime, let's switch to the post-game mixer in the gym. Let's take a look at some of the conversations going on. Over there in the line waiting for soft drinks is an interesting threesome: Ben, the star quarterback who just won the game with an awesome forty-five-yard pass; Megan, the homecoming queen; and Janet, a ninth-grade kid who likes mystery novels. It doesn't look like Janet is doing much talking. Even when Ben and Megan mention something to her or ask her a question, she kind of gives it a few words and stops.

Over there it looks like...yes, that's Spec, local computer whiz. He really is great with computers. In *his* opinion, he's *the* greatest; nobody at Microsoft can touch him. Next to him is Mr. Lange, one of the senior counselors, and a chaperon at the mixer. Since nobody else is talking to Spec at the moment, Mr. Lange is trying to start a brief conversation about Spec's college plans. Mr. Lange is one of the best senior counselors in the city. He knows college admissions backwards and forwards. Spec doesn't look like he's listening much, though.

What is shaping these conversations (or nonconversations)?

Images.

Janet sees herself as a nobody compared to Ben and Megan who, in her eyes, have social worth and status dripping from their pores. Why would they want to talk to *her*? They're probably just trying to be nice to the poor, so to speak. Actually, Ben and Megan don't feel that way at all; but Janet does, and until she changes her images, the conversation is going to be limited.

Spec, on the other hand, is so full of himself, so hyperconfident in his abilities and his success, that he sees little value in a conversation with Mr. Lange. Sure, Mr. Lange is a nice guy, but he doesn't know what it's like to make a computer sing, dance, and do cartwheels. At least Spec is pretty sure he doesn't, and that closes the door to conversation almost from the start because computers are all Spec is interested in.

Conversation with God is like that, too. We call it prayer. That's a fine word, but it doesn't change the fact that prayer is talking or communicating in some way with God. It will be shaped and colored, like any other communication, by the way you see yourself and the way you see God. Those are worth looking into.

What do you feel when you look into a mirror? What do you think of and feel when you see, hear, or think of "God"?

If you openly or secretly doubt your own goodness and worth, that can keep you from feeling that God really likes you, really believes in you, really wants your company and wants to listen to you.

On the other side, seeing yourself as one of the coolest, most talented, and independent people on earth can stand in the way of prayer, too. It's as though the image says, "I have friends who think I'm cool, somebody special who thinks I'm cute, a report card that says I'm smart, and a coach who says the team needs me" (or whatever the individual case might be). It's easy to draw the conclusion "What do I need God for? I'd lean on him if I needed to, but it doesn't look like I need to."

Wrong images of God stand in the way of good prayer, too. If God appears as a Grumpy Old Man, or a Meanest Judge in the County, that will keep you from talking to him any more often than you think you absolutely have to. You'll put off talking to him until you think you've been pretty good for quite some time—in other words, until you've put God back in a good mood.

If God looks like an Extremely Busy Distant Boss, you may also avoid trying to pray very often. It makes you feel like you're asking for an interview with the national Secretary of Education just to talk about the pencil sharpener in your homeroom that keeps chewing up pencils.

But nobody is too scroungy for God to like, nobody is too ordinary for God to be passionately interested in, and nobody is so cool that he or she doesn't need God. All of that directly goes against what God told us and against the in-the-flesh example of Jesus. He deliberately hung around ordinary, sinful people; he also told people they couldn't make it alone.

If prayer is a very small part of your life, give it another try. But like anything else, a thirty-second attempt at it every week or so isn't going to accomplish much. Things like learning to tie shoelaces take more effort than that.

Maybe try ten minutes a day if you're currently at less than that. Maybe divide it up, five minutes in the morning, five at night. Try some memorized prayers but concentrate on really meaning the words. And try some from-the-guts-of-your-life, let-it-all-spill-out communication, too. And leave time for listening.

Ten minutes a day. That's .0069444 of your time. A little less than 7 parts out of 1,000 in a 24-hour day.

CHAPTER TEN

Pig, Duck, or Cow:
Does It Depend?

"Who's to say what's right and what's wrong? You can't prove it; it's all just somebody's opinion, and everybody has a right to their opinion. I think it's a way some people use to control other people. They call something wrong and tell people not to do it because God said so, when actually they just want everybody to act like little robots. I think everybody should be free to decide for themselves what's right and wrong for them, and it might be totally different from the way somebody else thinks, but that's okay."

—Opinion of someone who has never been
robbed, beaten, used, cheated, vandalized,
lied to, lost a loved one to a drunk driver,
and so on

Being a little kid is nice in some ways. Things are pretty simple and unconfused. Look at how little kids learn about animals, for example. A couple of trips through *Our Animal Friends* and they've got it straight: This is a pig, that's a duck, that's a cow. This is a big pig, that's a little pig. There are no doubts, no questions about any of it. The book says so and so does Mommy. Case settled.

You don't question it as you grow older, either. You don't reach adolescence and begin to think, "That doesn't *always* have to be a cow. Sometimes it might be a gorilla, at least for some people. And what some people call a gorilla might be a cow to other people. It all depends." (Good luck to anyone who tries to get milk from a gorilla because, for him or her, it's a cow.)

Your understanding of right and wrong begins the same way: This is right, that is wrong. Why? Big people say so. Even when you're eating the cookies that Mom said to save for after dinner, you don't convince yourself that it's somehow a noble action, and that Mom will applaud once she begins thinking straight. You're just plain doing it anyway and hoping that Mom will actually believe the dog ate the cookies.

But unlike basic animal identification, the right/wrong picture *does* seem less clear as you grow older. You hear questioning from your peers ("So what's *wrong* with that?"), and sometimes their point of view seems to make sense. Many times it certainly seems more attractive. The question of *why* something is right or wrong comes up frequently: *What makes it that way?*

It's not a dumb question. It's a deep, intelligent question that people have wrestled with for ages. Actually, dumbness, more like dishonesty, enters the picture when people try very hard to answer the question *the way they want it* to be answered.

We can simplify the approaches to right and wrong down to three.

1. The Pig-Duck-Cow Approach. This action is right; that action is wrong. This action is moderately wrong; that action is horribly wrong. Why? Simply because it is what it is. End of discussion. If you're not certain about something, look it up in a book. It's all been decided.

2. The It-All-Depends Approach. Nothing is ever always right or always wrong. The only "always" is that you *always* have to look at the situation. Depending on circumstances, an action that's wrong at one time might be okay at some other time. All actions are like this; they all depend.

3. The Whatever-You-Think Approach. If you believe that something is wrong, and you do it, then it's wrong for you. But it wouldn't be wrong for somebody who doesn't think it's wrong.

Each one has a lot of truth in it and some major weaknesses.

The pig-duck-cow approach recognizes that some things just are what they are. Mass murder is mass murder; torture is torture; rape is rape. There's no way to make any of them okay, ever. You could more easily turn a banana into a space shuttle.

The it-all-depends approach recognizes that situations can sometimes change things. We're supposed to tell the truth, for example; that's the eighth commandment. But let's say your mother is an investigative reporter exposing organized crime in your city. One evening a large black car stops in front of your house. Two very large men with barely concealed guns show up on your front porch and ask where your mother is. They look about as friendly as an attack Doberman guarding its food dish. Are you obliged to tell these gentlemen the truth if you know it? Of course not. These guys don't want to find your mother so they can give her a certificate of appreciation. Telling the truth would put her life in danger; the situation changes the general rule.

The whatever-you-think approach recognizes that someone's *purpose* or *intention* can determine the morality of an action. For example, there's nothing wrong with putting sugar in someone's iced tea. But if you believe that a neighbor you can't stand is fatally allergic to sugar (even though he or she isn't), putting sugar in his or her iced tea becomes an act of attempted murder for you.

This approach also recognizes that a person's state of mind can affect how responsible people are for their actions in the eyes of God. A genuine condition of mental illness (which is different from a condition of being sort of upset) can drastically change a person's responsibility for his or her actions.

Those actions, however, may still be horrendously wrong and destructive. If a genuine madman sliced up someone you love, thinking that he or she was Satan, you wouldn't say, "Well, the attacker thought that this person I love was Satan, so actually it was a good thing to do, and it all works out for the best."

A balanced approach to right and wrong recognizes the truth in each of the above approaches *without making it the whole and only truth*. (It's often said that most errors are caused by trying to make one, single truth or even one, single, tiny grain of truth into *the one and only, rules-over-all truth*.)

Most people care far more about the morality, the right or wrongness of an action, when they're on the receiving end of it rather than the doing end of it. That's why Jesus said, "In everything do to others as you would have them do to you" (Matthew 7:12).

As a simple, practical approach for right and wrong—as a guideline for how to behave—one that covers just about everything—you can't find anything better. That's why it's called the Golden Rule.

If we all kept it, what a glorious and happy place this earth would be.

CHAPTER ELEVEN

. . . .

Life Preservers

"*F*or easy opening, simply pull drawstring across top of package."
"To open and use product, pull tab down and release E-Z Flo
spout. To close and store product safely, insert tab through reclosure
slot."
—Lies...all lies
"Align horizontal end of medium stabilizer bracket J-7 with opening on flange of side panel LL-4. Use slight pressure into flange until
bracket clicks. Using hex bolts WW-118, secure bracket to...."
—*Undoubtedly, one of the
things they do in hell*

Directions are not my favorite thing to read. You may have picked
that up. There are times when I'm convinced that how-to-assemble
directions in particular are written by demon-possessed people trying
to lure good, God-fearing people into cussing away all their holiness.

It's not that I'm *opposed* to directions as such; Lord knows, we
need them.

Imagine a coach announcing the plan for the game with the school's
number one archrival: "Here's the strategy; listen up: Go out there
and play like crazy. Score a lot. And don't let the other guys score.
Got it? Dismissed."

Imagine your history teacher on the first day of class: "The goal of
this course will be to study lots of events that happened in the past.
I'm going to let you on your own to do that because you're all intelligent people. I'll be back at the end of the semester to give the final

exam. The exam won't be easy, but if you study, you'll handle it well. Remember, learn as much about the past as you can. Class dismissed."

A TV chef: "The real secret of this casserole is in the baking. Set the temperature right where it should be—not too hot, not too cool. Don't bake it too long, but don't take it out too soon, either. Your family will absolutely love it! Thanks for watching; see you next week."

If you wanted to win that game, get an A in that course, or make that casserole for a special dinner, you'd be really—let's say—upset with the people in charge of the project. Their directions are about as helpful as a screwdriver when you need to sew on a button. General goals are fine. We need them, but we need particular, definite guidelines, too. An Eskimo who wants to visit Disney World needs more than the advice "Head south." That needs backing up with a detailed road map (or airline schedule), a list of places to stay, telephone numbers for making reservations, and quite a few other things to make the trip successful.

That's one of the reasons for the Ten Commandments and all the subtopics under them. They're directions for how to live during our journey of life. "Do good and avoid evil" is a great general direction, but we need more than that to make decisions about how to carry it out.

Unfortunately, the Commandments don't always have the image they deserve of a helpful road map or list of directions. Sometimes the image is something like "stuff I gotta do and even more stuff I'm not allowed to do."

So let's try doing away with them, and while we're at it, let's do away with all traffic laws. Wouldn't both driving and life in general be more fun? Do whatever you feel like, no matter what the feeling is or where it came from! Drive wherever you want, however you want, as fast as you want! What an all-day thrill!

More like what an all-day horror story.

The driving fun would end as soon as somebody decides to get some kicks by weaving in and out of all the lanes on a four-lane street at 75. Nobody would be crazy enough to do that? You know better. Remember that it's also no longer illegal to go through a six-pack of beer and get behind the wheel of a car right after that last can.

The "life in general" fun would also end quickly the moment any person or group of people more powerful than you decide to take and use your home, your possessions, your body, your family, your life. No use crying out, "Wait a minute: that's *wrong!*" because nothing is actually wrong anymore, remember? There are no don'ts anymore. There's no calling a law-enforcement officer because there is no more law enforcement because there are no more laws. At least none based on things like "Thou shalt not kill," "Thou shalt not steal," and so forth.

A few hours—maybe just a few minutes—of either driving or living without any laws would convince us of the reason for them.

At this point many people might say, "Well, sure, you'd have to have *some* laws, *some* commandments, but not all of them."

Which ones? Who's going to be in charge of deciding? What if they don't agree? Do we actually think we can do a better job of making rules for life than God, who created life?

The Commandments are there for the same reason as the lane dividers and speed-limit signs on the highway: Your life is valuable. Your family is valuable. Your plans and hopes and dreams for the future are valuable. Even your old Malibu is sort of valuable if it gets you to and from school or work.

We don't want any of them wrecked—which is going to happen a lot more easily if there are no driving laws.

Same way with life in general. Every good law that exists, beginning with the Commandments themselves, is there to protect something worthwhile, something valuable.

Sure, people break them. Does that mean we should do away with them?

Look at places in the world where every one is broken every day by most people.

What is life like there? Fun? Not for most people. Only for the wreckers of other people's lives, who are temporarily getting away with it. You don't want to be one of them, or one of their victims.

God doesn't want you to be, either. That's why God painted some lane dividers and put up some speed limit and other signs along the highway of life.

They're not "tests of obedience" to see if we're loyal enough to God to deserve a permanent vacation in heaven. They're the rules of a loving parent who doesn't want to see his kids bloodied up. When people keep them, life goes pretty well. When people routinely break them, life gets miserable.

We should be glad that they're there.

CHAPTER TWELVE

. . . .

The *S*-Word:
It's Not a Loch Ness Monster

"You don't look so good, Herb."

"Never felt better."

"Are you sure?"

"Absolutely. The doctor said I've got a tumor on my pancreas, but so what? I don't feel it."

"Herb, you're not making sense."

"Sure I'm making sense! I'm making sense for me, and that's what counts."

"What about the tumor?"

"I don't believe in 'em. It's a stupid outdated idea. Probably never was such a thing."

"What about what the doctor said?"

"Doctors—what do they know?"

You have this friend named Dave who just got a 61 percent on the biology midterm. There's more, unfortunately. His Spanish midterm was 68 percent, his history project got a 72 percent (not a complete wipeout, but not exactly good news either), and his English exam came back with a 57 percent at the top of the page.

Now you're known as wise and wonderful, so Dave comes to you for some comfort and insight. Which of the following would be best for him to hear?

- "Dave, you're an academic zero. You obviously don't have what it takes, and that's the plain darn sad truth. When they gave out brains, you must have been in the restroom. Either that, or you're an academic slob with such bad habits that there's no sense trying to change."

- "So *what,* Dave? What's a few grades? So you flunk some classes—does that change the wonderful person that you are? Does that mean you can never eat pizza or watch cartoons again? Of course not. Quit worrying. Besides, you passed *one* of them, and that 68 percent is an F *plus.*"

- "Gosh, I dunno, Dave. Bad news is bad for people. Gives 'em stress and stuff like that, you know? If I were you, I'd just not look at any more grades. When you get a paper back, just crumple it and toss it for two points in the corner can. Sure, there might be a 93 at the top of the page, but then again it might be a 39 instead, and you wouldn't want to see *that.* That could send you into a really bad depression or something. Just don't look from now on."

Okay, which piece of advice is it?

Right, they're all rotten. The correct answer is choice D, "none of the above." These three are very different, but they do have something in common: they *avoid what's real.* Whenever you try to avoid what's real, sooner or later you hit a brick wall. (Later isn't better than sooner, because by then you've built up a lot of speed—which makes for a bigger crash.)

It's like that with the *S*-word.

Sin. It's tempting to push the idea away, pretend there really is no such thing, or that if there is, it doesn't really matter. But that's avoiding what's real.

True, for some people, faith and religion are constant thinking about sin and degrees of sin and lists of sins. Mention the word "religion" to them, and they whip out a list of 9,435 things that are wrong to do and start preaching: "You-better-confess-shape-up-repent-renounce-your-evil-life-turn-yourself-around-or-God'll-wipe-you-out-with-a-bolt-of-lightning-one-of-these-days-better-believe-it-and-you'll-end-up-on-the-frying-pan-down-below-yessir-straight-to-hell-do-not-pass-Go-do-not-collect-a-thimble-of-ice-water!"

This was not exactly the message or the preaching style of Jesus. He did not go around preaching sin, doom, and hellfire all day long. Worrying about sin all day long is not a healthy religious attitude, and it's not what people of deep faith do.

But they don't tune it out, either. Nor did Jesus.

It's that other extreme that is more common today. It's the attitude that sin (if there really is such a thing) is no big deal and doesn't matter. Like dust in the air, it's all around, but so what? Being concerned about it is an old-fashioned, outdated religious hang-up.

Again, that simply ignores reality. All you have to do is look around at the injustice, suffering, and general garbage in the world. Read the crime and heartache headlines in the newspaper. That's not sin? It's just small stuff that doesn't matter? Don't tell that to the wife and kids of the man who gets killed in a convenience-store robbery.

A recent edition of our newspaper told the story of an honor student and outstanding athlete who was headed to a big-name college on a basketball scholarship until he was caught selling cocaine.

He had *not* previously been a drug dealer. Didn't use it, never sold it until he suddenly needed cash to pay for the abortions for two girls whom he had gotten pregnant.

Premarital sex → pregnancies → planned abortions → need for quick cash → drug dealing.

It doesn't end there; you know that. What about the two girls who undoubtedly feel immensely used and cheated on? Their boyfriend is no longer on his way to a sparkling basketball career; he's sitting in jail. What about the two, tiny, unborn kids? Will they get sliced apart and suctioned out in an abortion clinic anyway? The paper didn't say, of course. If they're carried and born, who's going to be their daddy?

And those individual occasions of sex that made the babies didn't happen out of nowhere. There almost certainly was peer pressure to score in order to be considered normal. Almost certainly there were messages from the media confusing sex and love. There may have been pornographic materials that made sex and multiple sex partners look like just any other piece of fun. There may have been influence from his own family background that made it seem like saving himself for marriage wasn't possible.

Of all the people who contributed to that pressure (and here we can include people like TV and movie producers), certainly none of them said or even thought, "Let's see if we can get a decent kid to treat relationships as something cheap, hire people to kill two of his unplanned babies, and end up selling drugs, to ruin his promising career and maybe his life."

But that's what happened.

A sinful action is never like a single dot on a piece of paper. It's more like one point in a complex, interconnected web.

We all live in that web. Because of Jesus, we don't have to get trapped in it and destroyed by it. The first thing we need to do, though, is to admit reality: admit that the web's around us, and admit that our sinful actions both result from it and contribute to it. Sin is not a Loch Ness monster: maybe it exists, maybe not, and even if it does, we don't need to worry about it because it's not going to climb out of there and destroy people. Sin can and does destroy people, including people who seem to be having a lot of fun while the destruction is going on.

Admitting sin, remember, does not mean getting hung up on it and seeing ourselves as worthless. It's simply facing reality and then turning to the healing forgiveness of our Savior.

CHAPTER THIRTEEN

Morality Is Not
Just a Weird Apple Pie

To be or not to be.
   To use regular mustard or hot spicy mustard.
To cheat or not to cheat.
To rent a couple videos and have some people over, or to find a place with open bowling and ask some friends if they want to go.
To do a research paper on the French Revolution or on the War of the Roses.
To paint the living room Antique White or Outrageous Orange.
To be or not to be...sexually active.
How many categories of decisions?

Elvira stood in the kitchen, tense and trembling, her hand curled around the bottle of catsup. *"Don't do it!"* said a voice from somewhere deep within her. *"It's against everything you know, everything you learned. Your grandmother would die if she knew!"*

She glanced at the oven dial, which she had already set to 480 degrees, then over at her freshly made but unbaked apple pie. *"No!"* came the voice again. *"Turn the oven down! Put the catsup back in the fridge!"*

Time and again Elvira had made wonderful, good, beautiful apple pies. She never would have considered what she was on the verge of doing if it weren't for Blankford. *Blankford.* The very thought of his name sent throbbing pulses through her lonely cardiovascular system. At first he had simply been her boss; now he was her boyfriend, too, and would there be more? Wedding bells? He was perfect in every way but one. He loved apple pie covered with a thick layer of spicy catsup and baked to a burnt crisp. He had said so once again as he accepted her invitation to dinner.

It was a horrible, terrible way to bake an apple pie. Elvira knew that. But she wanted her job and companionship and love. Maybe this time for those reasons it wouldn't be so wrong. Maybe not wrong at all.

Let's stop here before we need to swallow half a roll of literary antacids. You can finish Elvira's story yourself if you like. She's fictional, invented to illustrate conflict between two things: *I know* (how to make a good apple pie) vs. *I want* (a job, a relationship).

In this story, the only thing at stake is normal vs. kinky apple pie. But let's say Elvira is real, and this time her boyfriend/boss wants her to fix some payroll records to hide several thousand dollars he stole from the company. What if he wants her to spread a vicious rumor about his rival for a promotion? What if he wants some casual sex after office hours?

Then it becomes a *moral* conflict. It has the same ingredients: *I know* or I'm rather certain that a certain action is wrong. Doing it will get me something that *I want* because it seems to fill needs that I have.

Unlike Elvira's charred, catsup-crisped apple pie, wrong things do not always look disgusting. In fact, just like the forbidden fruit in Genesis, they often look pretty good. People don't say to themselves, "This is a disgusting, stomach-turning, barf-inducing, putrid thing to do; therefore, I will go for it." Usually they convince themselves that because something *looks* good (fun, profitable, whatever), it can't really *be* very bad, maybe not bad at all.

Especially not this time. That's the BUT part.

Elvira knows this is not how to make a good, decent apple pie. BUT since it may add to her job security, boyfriend security, and possible future happiness, *this time* maybe it's okay. And again, that's fine, no harm done, when we're dealing with apple pie. But when we're dealing with moral choices, with right and wrong, we can't operate that way.

It's called "rationalizing." It means convincing yourself that something wrong is really okay *this* time, here and now, in these circumstances, because of these particular factors, and so on.

Do *circumstances* ever change the morality of an action? Of course. Knocking someone senseless with a baseball bat is an extremely evil action. But if a gunman is about to pull the trigger of a .38 on an innocent victim, and you just happen to be standing behind the gunman without his knowing it, and you've got this baseball bat handy, the situation is radically different.

Notice how major and how unusual the circumstances are to justify the use of the baseball bat. The fact that someone insults you, or your boyfriend or girlfriend, is not a circumstance that makes it okay. Neither is the fact that he or she has been nasty and on your case for weeks.

By now you've caught on that the chapter opening contains two major kinds of decisions: moral (right/wrong) and others. At least one of them really does "depend": if it's *your* living room in *your personal* home, and you have a passion for vivid, violent, knock-the-dentures-down-your-throat orange, you have every right to paint it that, and it's no more a moral choice than deciding what brand of detergent to use.

If you live with several other people, whom you know are going to be irritated and upset by the color every time they enter the room, painting it that becomes an act of aggression.

Recognizing and deciding moral conflicts is one of the things that separate us from animals. A pack of wild jackals doesn't stop to discuss the fairest way to divide up an animal they've just killed for dinner. The strongest and meanest get the most.

We're human. We're different. We're called by God to do what we know is right.

CHAPTER FOURTEEN

You're Responsible
for Your Beeper

"Your honor, my client cannot be held responsible for his actions. True, they were unfortunate, but responsibility is a different matter, and in that regard, he stands before you innocent."

"And how is that so, counselor?"

"His beeper didn't work, your honor."

"His...did you say his BEEPER didn't work?"

"Exactly, your honor. No beeper, therefore no chance to respond to the beeper, therefore no responsibility for the actions."

"But isn't it HIS beeper?"

"Well, yes it is. Nevertheless, IT simply didn't BEEP. No beep, no responsibility. I know this man, your honor: If it had beeped, he would not have done these things."

The old science-fiction and horror movies had some standard plots. One of them was the implanted-device plot. A bad guy, like an evil scientist or a junior-high biology genius out for revenge because everybody laughed at him, implanted a device in somebody. Normally, this implanted person would be as sweet as Grandma serving apple pie. But when the device was activated, it made the person do nasty things, like destroy New York City, force innocent people to eat raw broccoli and write research papers, and so forth.

Sometimes we see *conscience* that way, only in reverse.

Conscience is sometimes called "that little voice that tells you when you're doing something wrong" (or did something wrong or are about to do something wrong.) We say that somebody's conscience is bothering him or her, or that our conscience won't let us do something. Or that our conscience didn't mind if we did something or doesn't mind if we're planning something. "My conscience ain't bothering *me*."

There's some truth in all that. Some. But it's not the whole story.

Definitely, *conscience* is what tells us right from wrong. That's what the word means, and it's an okay definition. But conscience is not an implant. It's not something apart from us, separate from us, some little compartment tucked away in a corner of our brain.

If it were, then the defense attorney's argument in our opening example would make sense. If the beeper doesn't beep, you can't answer the phone call; if the conscience doesn't beep, buzz, clang, gong, or stick a needle in a sensitive emotional area, then a person can't be responsible for what he or she did. The conscience didn't work, so the actions must be *its* fault.

That makes about as much sense as the following:

"Jake, I've got to take you out of the lineup. You haven't hit the ball in twenty times at the plate; the last time up you swung at a pitch a half foot over your head."

"My eyes weren't working right, Coach. They didn't let me see where that pitch was coming in."

"You let a ground ball going about half a mile an hour roll right through your feet."

"My arm didn't function correctly, Coach. It just didn't reach down to the right spot. Believe me, I *wanted* to field that ground ball."

"You're supposed to be playing third base, but you spent most of the last inning at the hot dog stand."

"It's my sense of direction, Coach. It gets screwed up sometimes, and it doesn't let me see where I'm supposed to be. I even remember thinking that I probably wasn't supposed to be at the hot dog stand right then, but...well, like I said, it's that dumb sense of direction. I guess I was born with it. Anyway, I hope you can see that none of this is my fault. You can't blame me when I was born with these things that don't always work right."

It's possible for a person to have a physical condition that prevents operating the way he or she would really like to. But that doesn't sound like the case here. It sounds as if Jake is trying to paint himself as something completely separate from his muscles, his eyes, and almost anything else that might be the occasion of some blunder. It's not much different from the fifth-grade classroom excuse "My arm must have swung out by accident, and I guess it hit him."

Point is, you can, well, train your arm not to do that.

Conscience, our sense of right and wrong, is like that. It's not an implant, completely separate from *us*. It's an ability, a skill, that we have *and that we're responsible for developing correctly,* just as a baseball player is responsible for developing his or her ability to tell whether or not the pitch is worth hitting.

Let's use that as an example because probably everyone has held a bat in his or her hand and tried to hit a baseball or a softball. It won't be a perfect example, but it'll work.

Nobody is expected to judge the pitch perfectly and get a hit every time at bat. But you *are* expected to work at it. If you don't really try to judge the ball, don't really study the situation, don't bother learning or even looking at the third-base coach's signals, just swing when you feel like swinging and stand there when you feel like standing there, then you're responsible for at least some of the failures that will certainly happen. You're expected to try to develop the ability to judge pitches correctly.

Conscience is like that. It's an ability to judge—not incoming pitches and whether they're worth swinging at or not, but actions and whether they're right to do or not.

Now if you're not on a baseball or softball team, you have no obligation to learn how to judge incoming pitches. There's no obligation to play on a team.

But life as part of the human race is a team you're on automatically. True, you didn't choose it, but it's not likely you want to get off it either. Being on the team roster carries some responsibilities.

Developing the ability to judge right from wrong, and acting accordingly, is one of the biggest.

CHAPTER FIFTEEN

• • • • • • • • • • •

So Many Voices

"Getcher snow cones right here!"

"Hurry, this offer is limited."

"Make no mistake about it, folks, we've got all prices beat!"

"Don't miss this chance to own a brand new...."

"...and the beautiful thing about this All-Purpose Kitchen Helper is that...."

"Attention, shoppers! Be sure to visit the sporting goods department and check out our spectacular unadvertised specials!"

Who do you listen to? (And if only LIFE's choices were this simple.)

Author: This is pretty good. It's chapter 15, and you're still hanging in. We haven't even had any love scenes or car chases or...

Reader: You're going to have love scenes and car chases?

Author: We can if you'd like. Here:

> Samantha leaned over in the cab of the sixteen-wheeler and turned her trembling lips toward Alexander. "Whatever happens, you know I love you," she said. He smiled, leaned over, and kissed her as his sinewy biceps turned the steering wheel of the massive semi, wrestling the huge vehicle around the hairpin turn of Route 47. He had pushed the laws of physics to their limit, but successfully. Behind them, the shiny black Lincoln filled with organized-crime hit men was not so successful.

The Lincoln veered off the road, hit a rose bush, and burst into a huge inferno of orange flame and black smoke.

How was that?

Reader: Do I have to give an opinion?

Author: No. Might be better if you didn't.

Reader: Are you sure you didn't lecture a little bit here and there?

Author: I guess. Sometimes it goes with the territory. This isn't easy, you know.

Reader: What isn't?

Author: Being an adult. At least if you're an adult who gives a darn. It gets you into some tricky balancing acts.

Reader: What do you mean?

Author: Trying to talk or write about things you know you've learned, and you know they're for real, not stuff you imagined or just wished were true, and that you deeply care about because you're convinced they're important, and that you want to pass on to younger people because you care about them, too. *And* you want to do all this without sounding superior or narrow-minded, or like you're on some kind of cheap power trip.

It has nothing to do with being smarter or better. It's nothing more than having lived longer. If somebody gets to be forty or fifty or sixty and hasn't picked up *some* things for certain that he or she didn't realize at fifteen or twenty, that person has been sleepwalking through life.

Reader: Why can't every generation just figure it all out for themselves?

Author: You going to have kids?

Reader: I think so.

Author: Are you going to tell them to look for cars before they cross the street? Not to take candy from strangers?

Reader: Sure.

Author: You could let them find out from experience.

Reader: Okay, so you tell kids some basics. Things that are really important.

Author: Such as?

Reader: That'll depend a little on who's talking. Not everybody agrees on what's important. What's the point here?

Author: Exactly what you just said. A lot of life comes down to who you listen to. Not that you don't or shouldn't have any mind of your own, but most of us don't stay up late at night making notes and outlines of what's important to human existence. It might not be a bad idea, but we seldom do it. We listen to other people, toss what they say around in our minds, add some things of our own, and come out with a mixture that we use to live by. Even with deep thinkers, a lot of what they arrive at came in some form or other from other people. A lot depends on who you listen to. Especially when you're forming your conscience.

Reader: Sounds like you're about to give me a list of approved sources.

Author: Absolutely. Here it comes: Mom, Dad, Grandma, Grandpa, teachers, pastors, sometimes Aunt Helen. That about covers it.

Reader: You *are* joking again, right?

Author: Yeah. Also, I left out God.

Reader: But doesn't God talk through people sometimes?

Author: Lots. Which brings us back to the same idea: Who do you listen to? God might be talking through some of them, and really foul...—let's call it garbage—might be slithering out of some others.

Reader: How do you tell the difference?

Author: Great question. Find a 100-percent foolproof, failproof answer to that one, write it up or film it in a way that will persuade everyone to follow it, distribute it to the world, and you'll change the course of the human race for the better.

Reader: So trying to tell the difference is pretty hopeless?

Author: Not at all. You can up the odds by getting rid of some prejudices, automatic reactions, stuff like that.

Reader: For example?

Author: Like the prejudice that when an older person gives an opinion, especially a warning about wrong things or danger of some kind, it's not worth taking too seriously because people like that don't understand the *real* world anymore, and they've forgotten how to have fun.

Reader: Things aren't right just because an adult says them.

Author: Bingo. I wouldn't trust some adults to give me advice on how to use a paper clip if I needed it. But you can look at the track record a person has, actually no matter what age that person is. Sometimes we're influenced by people whose past history and track record practically scream out, "I'm messed up; don't take my advice for anything!" But because these people can also be cute, sexy, clever, exciting to be with, or socially powerful, or because they give us things we like, it's easy to follow them anyway.

Reader: You have an example?

Author: *An* example? More than I like to think about. I'll just do one, though.

A girl I had taught was telling me about her boyfriend. Now I'm not saying the guy was total scum, Satan in person, and so forth. But here was his track record: dropped out of school; arrested three times; spent a short jail term for one of them; obvious alcohol and marijuana habit on the verge of becoming even heavier; trouble holding even entry-level, burger-flipping jobs for very long. And she wanted to *marry* him. Why? "But sometimes he can be *so sweet.* He's really nice when you get to know him." I get scared whenever I hear that line: "But he can be so sweet at times."

Reader: So what happened?

Author: She has a child she can't care for, a drinking problem she can't handle, and a part-time, going-nowhere job that she hates. The boyfriend—former boyfriend—isn't in the picture.

It's not that there wasn't anybody else around giving different advice. It's all a matter of who you listen to.

Reader: Okay. Some things turn out rotten, I know that. Sounds a little like a scare story, though.

Author: It *is* a scary story.

Reader: What if you really aren't sure who to listen to, though? That guy should have been pretty obvious. It's not always that obvious.

Author: Then you do an obvious thing we haven't mentioned yet. You take the case, the decision, whatever it is, to somebody who *does* know for sure. Somebody with, let's say, a perfect track record.

Reader: You're talking God.

Author: Exactly. I've never met anybody smarter.

Reader: What do you say?

Author: "Show me what to do. Please show me what to do." About a hundred or so times, maybe more. Not because God is zoned out and you have to get God's attention, but because sometimes it takes that many times of saying it to actually mean it. Sometimes we ask people, God included, what we should do, but there's really only one answer we want to hear.

It also helps to describe the entire situation as part of the prayer, every detail, including our feelings. Again, it's not that God is clueless about it. Putting it in the prayer helps *us* see it more clearly.

Reader: This is a long chapter.

Author: I can take a hint.

CHAPTER SIXTEEN

Fony Phreedom

It's Easter Sunday morning, and Jesus is walking by the tomb. He looks in and sees someone sitting there in the gloom.

"Hey, come on out!" he calls. "I've risen from the tomb to new life and brought you with me."

"No, thanks," the person answers. "I think I'll just stay here. Thanks anyway."

"But there's a whole new life out here!" Jesus exclaims. "Why would you want to stay there in the dark? You can hardly move around in there!"

"I've gotten accustomed to it," the person answers. "It's comfortable. I enjoy it here. Usually."

You've seen this supermarket scene many times. It's repeated daily at supermarkets throughout the nation. The characters are Little Kid (maybe between three and ten) and Parent (older than that).

Parent and Kid approach checkout lane. Kid wants candy, grabs a bar or a bag or a box and puts it in shopping cart. Parent tells Kid he or she has already had enough candy, and besides, there's some at home. Parent puts candy back on display shelf and begins unloading cart.

Kid re-grabs candy and puts it back in cart with the simple, obvious objection, "But I *want* it!"

Parent says, "Now you heard what I said" and again replaces candy.

Two seconds later, people in nearby aisles jerk to attention and ask one another, "Isn't that the tornado-warning siren? But it's not even cloudy outside." Actually, it's Kid expressing strong opinion about wanting candy. Spectacular audio show is accompanied by several pints of fake tears.

Parent finally says, "Well, *just one,* but you can't eat it now. You'll have to wait until after supper."

Kid instantly recovers from extreme emotional trauma, opens candy, and begins chomping. Parent suddenly adopts the personality of a TV wrestling referee and somehow does not notice; he or she continues to empty shopping cart.

You have to feel sorry in a way for the kid, who is learning a disastrous lesson: "If I really want something, I simply act like a brat, break the rules, and sooner or later I'll get it, even if it's something I shouldn't have."

Sometimes that lesson sticks around and becomes a regular way of looking at life long after the kid is no longer a kid. At sixteen or eighteen or twenty-five or older, he or she won't scream, cry fake tears, or jump up and down. The methods will change, but the attitude doesn't.

"I want; therefore, I will get." It's easy to recognize that attitude and see how immature and harmful it is when we're looking at a little kid at the supermarket.

If that same attitude is at work in ourselves, it's a lot harder to see it. After all, we're not five years old anymore. Shouldn't we be free to decide for ourselves if and when and how much candy we're going to have?

But the candy is just a symbol for anything that looks good, tastes good, feels good. A lot of it's okay, and a lot of it isn't. That's life. That's reality.

Does following a code of right and wrong restrict our freedom? Sure, if we define freedom as being able to do anything that looks like a kick. But that's not what it means. Sooner or later that kind of "freedom" will knock holes in somebody else's life or health or reputation or property, and our own as well. Real freedom doesn't cramp or destroy other people's freedom, or violate their right to enjoy a safe, happy life.

You can get trapped in that kind of "freedom," too.

Here's Joe Free and Cool. Nobody gonna tell *him* what to do. Especially if they tell him he'd better ease off the alcohol and the grass. He runs his own life and doesn't want to hear about anything that would restrict his freedom.

So he tries to handle school and getting regularly high at the same time.

This means sometimes scrambling to cover for cut classes, scrambling to copy homework at the last minute, walking into tests he doesn't know anything about and hoping he can either fake or cheat enough to pass (without getting caught). It means hiding evidence, lying about where he's been and hoping the lies are convincing or don't get found out, maybe lifting a little money here and there to cover expenses, and always thinking, often worrying, about covering his tracks well enough.

That's freedom?

If every time I see something attractive, a spoiled little kid inside me starts screaming, "I want!" and won't shut up and give me peace until I figure out a way to get it, legally or illegally, morally or immorally, that's not being free. It may look like it at first, but it's not.

It's more like living in the tomb in our opening parable. Even though it's a tomb, it can become so familiar, so much a part of a person's life, that he or she will refuse invitations to leave it even though leaving it means coming out into *real* freedom.

Sometimes people get into tomb-dwelling from listening to the GET-IT-NOW messages that fill our society. We're often told that we deserve anything we want as soon as we want it. Psychologists call it "instant gratification," and a whole array of products, even complete industries, have been built around it.

"BUY NOW; PAY LATER!" Lots of financial tombs get started that way. No problem with putting some things on a card, but when you start signing up for everything you want that way, financial reality bites back.

Beautiful hair, gorgeous body, popularity, wealth, health, and happiness: you can get it all easily and quickly, according to some advertising message or other. And the idea rubs off that nothing should wait, that *you* should never have to wait. Not for money, not for sex, not for anything.

Now combine that with the idea that everything is disposable. We have disposable diapers, disposable gloves, disposable containers for almost everything. The only caution—and that's fairly recent—is "Please dispose of properly."

That rubs off, too: Everything is disposable. Relationships are disposable: just tell whoever it is to take a walk. Babies are disposable: just make an appointment with an abortion clinic. Mistakes are disposable. There's no actual advertisement for that, but the idea comes through along with everything else.

It all produces the conclusion that you go for what you want because you have a right to have it *now,* and if you screw something up along the way, no problem: It's disposable.

All in the name of being free to do, have, get whatever you want. But that's a phony freedom.

Real freedom helps you genuinely grow. Real freedom brings you peace. Real freedom doesn't give you a quick thrill, then make you pay for it. Real freedom doesn't open a small door, then slam a big one shut in your face.

Real freedom is the kind Jesus taught.

And sometimes it means accepting a *no.* That's reality, that's life, and over a lifetime, that's happiness.

CHAPTER SEVENTEEN

. . . .

You Only Live (and Die, Too) Once

"You like your job?"

"It's okay. _____ [name of another former student] works there, too. You remember him?"

"Sure. He was just a couple years older than you. My memory isn't THAT gone. Is he still going with _____ [name of another former student]?"

"That was ages ago. He's going mostly with Bud Lite and Jack Daniels now."

"He's really got a problem?"

"Probably."

*—Actual conversation in
my kitchen five days ago*

You may or may not be into the Car Thing, which means seeing cars, certain favorite models of cars in particular, as just a step or two below a beautiful body of the opposite sex. That's probably more a guy thing than a girl thing, but in any case either you own a car or you soon will. Eventually, you'll almost certainly need one to get to school, work, or college classes.

Let's imagine that you own not just a car, but the ultimate driving machine—whatever that is for you because it'll be different for different people. Some would choose a luxury-status thing like a Rolls or a BMW. Some would go for a state-of-the-automotive-art racing machine. Some might want a classic collector's item like a '57 Chevy. There would be limo lovers and truck fans. I'd want my original '66

Mustang back. In any case, we're pretending that you own your ultimate set of dream wheels.

Now imagine something else. A friend encourages you to enter it in the Random Rodeo. You've heard of car and truck rodeos before, but not this one. You ask about it. He or she explains:

People bring their cars to this huge empty lot where the rodeo takes place. But they don't actually drive their cars themselves. A tiny computer is installed in each car. It "drives" the car in random, unpredictable fashion. Forward, backward, right, left, U-turns, idles, and full throttles—you can never tell what the computer is going to make the car do.

In the process, of course, cars occasionally flip over while turning too fast. Transmissions sometimes get ripped apart by being thrown into reverse at high speeds. Occasionally, cars smash into one another and get totaled. But that's all part of the show.

You ask if any *people* get hurt in addition to the cars getting damaged.

Not often, your friend explains. Oh, sure, a couple weeks ago this one car went really crazy and rammed through the fence, and a couple of people who were "just in the wrong place at the wrong time" are in bad shape now. But that was just that one time. Some people have been bringing their cars there pretty often, and nothing bad has happened so far.

You figure there must be incredible prizes for, well, for something, to make up for this kind of risk.

"There's no *prize*, man. It's just fun to do. And all the people there are cool people. If you bring your car to the rodeo, they'll think you're cool too."

If there were such a thing, would you enter your car?

Not likely. You know it would be truly stupid. If you got the car as a gift, it would be an insult to the person who gave it to you. And, yes, it's just plain wrong. Especially when lives, as well as fine machinery, are at risk, it's just plain wrong.

Most people would never risk putting their *cars* out of control like that. But many do it with their bodies, their lives, and other people's lives by putting themselves out of control with chemicals.

You don't have to be an alcoholic or addict to wreck something. All you have to do is be under the influence. It doesn't matter whether you drank it, smoked it, shot it up, huffed it, or for that matter soaked in it.

Young people are turned off by alcohol- and drug-education messages that suggest addiction is automatic and practically at hand from the moment someone takes the first drink, smokes the first partial joint, or whatever the experiment is. You know that's not true, although frighteningly quick addiction *really is* possible, depending on a person's individual body chemistry. It happens more often than most of us realize.

But the point remains that you don't have to be an addict to ruin something or have something ruined. All you have to do is lose some inhibitions at a time when you really need them.

An "inhibition" is a feeling, a judgment call or "little voice" inside you, that says, "Better not." Like anything else, inhibitions can be too strong, rule your life with fear, and keep you from trying anything more risky than eating spaghetti or watching cartoons. They can keep you from voicing your opinion in a group, trying out for a sport, or asking someone to a dance.

But they provide warnings you do need, warnings of things that *are* genuinely stupid, genuinely wrong, genuinely and unnecessarily dangerous. You don't want to stifle them completely, even for just a little while, and that's what alcohol and other drugs will do. A few drinks will shut up the voice that normally says, "This is a dangerous and seriously dumb idea; back off before you screw something up." A few drinks will shut up the voice that normally says, "That is flat out *wrong*" and sets loose a different voice that says, "Hey, *live a little* for once!"

Lots of people have died because of the alcohol/drug-inspired voice that said, "Live a little."

Some in car wrecks. Some from gang-related activities. Some in daredevil stunts. Some from AIDS.

You have more and better than a magnificent vehicle, and you received it as a free, loving gift: your body, your mind, your life. You don't get another set. Putting them temporarily out of control with chemicals is a risk that's both simply stupid and simply wrong.

· · · · · · · · · · · ·

Sex
(No Need for Fancy Titles Here)

"I'm telling you: Don't go over the back fence into the woods, understand?"

"Why not?"

"Crocodiles live back there! Wild crocodiles! They're mean and vicious and always hungry, and they wait where you can't see them for somebody to come by, especially little kids. They like to chew up little kids better than anything else!"

"Are you sure?"

"Of course I'm sure. They ate two little kids just last week. You should learn a lesson from them. They knew they shouldn't go over the fence, but they did anyway, and now they're DEAD!"

"But it's so pretty back over the fence."

"That doesn't stop the crocodiles."

> *—A really stupid thing to tell a kid.*
> *Unless, of course, the crocodiles and*
> *the dead kids are absolutely real.*

Very few things—maybe no other single thing—will bring you as much joy or as much pain as sex. When you're dealing with something that powerful, it makes a lot of sense to think about it ahead of time. Let's start there.

Too many conversations and classes about sex amount to adults saying, "Don't!" and young people saying, "Why not?" Or the adults say, "Well, be responsible and careful," and the young people say, "What do you think we are, idiots?" And that's sort of the end of it, even though the whole process may have taken several days or even weeks. I hope we can do better than that.

Let's go back to the starting statement. Maybe it's not true of everybody. Maybe for some people, winning or losing in athletic competition or in business competition brings more joy or more pain than sex. But for many of us, it's sex, and for those who think I'm reducing most of life to the bedroom or the back of the Chevy van, let me explain some things.

Even though we said, "Sex," what we're really talking about here is a much bigger thing called sexuality, and that takes in a couple universes more than simply uniting a set of male and female body parts. But it's the attraction leading up to that uniting that brings in everything else.

Figure it. Figure the bad news first because that shows how good the good news is.

Rape. Prostitution. Pornography. Sexual slavery. Child molesting. Unwanted and abandoned babies and kids. More than twenty-five sexually transmitted diseases, some leading to death. Divorce. Abortion. Murder (people kill over romance and sex).

Add to that all the broken hearts, shattered dreams, and wrecked lives connected with each of the above.

Put it all together and you've got enough foul, putrid, stinking garbage to make you gag nonstop for several lifetimes. And every last bit of it could have been eliminated if there were no such thing as sexual attraction, romance, sexual union itself. Every last bit of it would be gone and out of the picture if there were no such thing as sexuality.

(How would the human race continue? God is God and could have set up dozens of other ways to make more people.)

Really think of this: All that incredible mountain of pain, suffering, regret, and gag-you-to-death garbage would be *gone* without this sex thing.

God made sex anyway.

Didn't have to.

Did anyway. Why?

Why? God doesn't *have* to do anything. God does things for reasons. There's only one possibility:

Sex—not just clothes-off-bed-or-family-room-floor-or-back-of-the-van time, but everything else that goes before and with and beyond it—is so wonderful, *so beautiful when it goes right,* when it goes the way God planned and designed it, that *it was worth taking the risk* of all the other garbage (I can think of a blunter, more colorful word, and I'm sure you can too).

All the stuff that people mention when they talk about crocodiles. There are two kinds of crocodile stories.

Let's say I don't want my kid to go over the back fence simply because *I* never did. Or maybe it's because I want to control my kid and make him or her turn out exactly like me. So I invent these scary but imaginary reptilian bogeymen to control my kid's behavior. That's not right, not honest.

But *if there really are crocodiles,* then telling crocodile stories isn't a cheap scare tactic. It's being a basic, decent parent, or whatever my role is. If I keep my mouth shut about crocodiles just because I know my kid doesn't like to hear about them, then I'm a wimpy excuse for a parent or whatever role I'm supposed to be filling. There's a huge difference between a cheap scare story and a scary story that's real.

There *are* crocodiles over there in Do-It Land. We'll mention some of them because I refuse to offer you anything other than reality. But for now, let's look at a different kind of story.

Call them Jack and Jill. They meet and find each other interesting. They date, have fun, begin to care a lot about each other, and learn more about each other. It's now a lot more and deeper than the fact that Jill has a great shape and Jack has dynamite pecs, or whatever first caught their attention. It's more than liking the same kind of pizza or agreeing that parents are weird sometimes. This is love.

And the idea of making love looks really great. Obviously. They're normal young people.

But they don't. As much as they truly love each other right now, they know that marriage and a whole life together is not automatic or right around the corner. But if the relationship does lead there, "all the way" to marriage, they want a unique, totally special, all-the-way way to celebrate it. So they wait.

And get married.

And learn together. Just them. No regrets, memories, or comparisons from the past to bring to bed with them. No concerns about viruses or bacteria or physical conditions picked up in some other bedroom. Just them—their bodies, their hearts, their love.

Cool.

Not that any marriage that doesn't begin that way is doomed, or that the people are bad or cheap. Not saying that at all.

Still, the way God designed it, that's both cool and beautiful.

CHAPTER NINETEEN

· · · · · · · · · · · ·

Sex II

"Daddy, what's this for?"

"That turns the car on and makes the motor go rummm-rummm. Don't try it, though, okay?"

"What's that for?"

"That makes the car go backward or forward."

"What's that other thing for?"

"That's to make it warm in the car if it's cold outside or cool if it's hot outside."

"What's the car for?"

"The car is for...you know, no one's ever asked me that! That's a good question."

"Do you know the answer?"

"Sure. The car is for going bye-bye."

If only "What is sex for?" were that simple.

"If I had a hammer, I'd hammer in the morning, / I'd hammer in the evening / all over this land."

Sixties trivia time: Who sang that? Who wrote it? Ask your par...no, maybe ask your grandparents. Correct answers win sets of love beads and tie-dyed bell-bottoms.

What's a hammer for? You can use it for many things, obviously, some good, some not. You could list them along a line ranging from awful to wonderful:

awful ⬅————————————➡ wonderful

killing people ⬅———➡ building a home for people you love

Sex isn't *exactly* like that, but we can use that model to talk about it.

You can use sex for horrible reasons that use and hurt people and tear lives apart. You can use sex to build and celebrate a lifelong relationship of growing married love that gets better and deeper and better and deeper.

What should you do with it? What's it for? Things are *for something*. More importantly, *people* are *for something*. It's called purpose. If we don't believe that at all, then we end up with the idea that whatever anybody wants to do with anything or anybody is okay as long as they can get the job done.

Is that how you want somebody seeing you and your body? Not likely.

But that's an extreme position. Most people aren't there. So we come back to the main question: What is sex for? What does it mean?

- A simple, self-centered, turn-on-the-sexual-nerve-endings thrill, just another but more-exciting-than-average way to have fun?
- A way of showing somebody that you like being with them and want them to stay with you?
- A technique to feel powerful or worthwhile?
- A pleasure trip you give to someone and he or she gives to you—with no expectations, just a favor you do for each other?
- A way to deal with boredom, loneliness, or stress?
- A way of keeping someone in a relationship, even though the relationship doesn't have much else going for it, but you hope sex will make something else, like love, happen or re-happen?
- A beautiful (and exciting) expression of love for the person you've joined yourself to in marriage? And an opportunity to do the most awesome thing a human being can ever do: *help create another human being?*

Some people would say, "All of the above, depending on the people and the circumstances." Sounds like a sensible answer until you realize that it's the same as saying "all of the above" (the violent through the beautiful) in answer to "What's a hammer for?"

In searching for an answer to the "What is sex for?" question, you have two basic ways to go: look for and accept what the inventor of sex says (that's God) or what somebody/anybody else says. And God's words are not exactly mysterious. There's really no, "Gosh, what on earth does God *mean?*" about it.

It's one of the first things you find in the Bible, at least if you start at the beginning with Genesis. Chapter 2: "The man" (in many translations traditionally known as "Adam") has been given the task of naming all the animals. And he does, but he gets bored silly. Not hard to understand: some animals are interesting and cute, but you can't hold much of a conversation with them, and cuddling up with a hippo isn't likely to give you a nice warm glow.

So God makes Eve. Adam wakes up, sees her standing there, and says what amounts to, "Now *this is more like it!*" (Genesis 2:23).

Right there, at that first, very obvious point of open sexuality (they're both naked, remember) comes the answer to what sex is for: "Therefore a man leaves his father and his mother and clings to his *wife,* and they become one flesh" (Genesis 2:24, emphasis added).

"One flesh": a very physical and wonderful expression, and there's not much doubt about what it includes. But the word is *wife.* Sex is intended to build and strengthen a loving, lifelong relationship between husband and wife. That's literally what it's for.

Does everybody believe and practice that? Of course not. People often don't follow what God said about truth and honesty, either. The point is that there isn't much doubt about God's directions.

And now *the* question that always arrives at this point: "But if you really love the other person, doesn't that make it okay? What's wrong with it if you love someone?"

That's not a stupid nor merely rebellious question. If two people have sex out of real, genuine love (maybe it's not the deepest possible level, but it's real), doesn't that change things?

Sure it does. Only a moral idiot would say otherwise. Take these two situations:

1. Jack is tired of listening to other guys' score-stories without having one of his own. Besides, he wonders what sex is like; actually, he's wondered that for years. He watched a porno video along with some other guys at a party last year, and the people in it looked like they were going nuts with fun. He's been going with Jill for a couple months, and he decides it's time to make a hit.

Jill is likewise tired of being known as a freeze among some of her classmates. On top of that, she hasn't been getting along very well with her mother lately, and her mother keeps preaching about being a "good girl," so sex looks like a really good way to express some independence, even though her mother isn't going to know about it.

So they do it.

Jack tells Jill that he really cares about her, Jill says the same thing about Jack, and they do it. Jack feels like a real man, Jill feels like a real woman, and they can both show up at school on Monday with "lucky weekend" smiles on their faces.

Incredibly, dirt-sucking cheap.

2. Jack and Jill have been dating for three years. Broke up briefly a couple times, but got back together. They're way beyond just thinking the other person is cute, although they certainly haven't stopped thinking that. They've spent hours upon hours of getting to know each other. They've counseled, cared for, helped, and healed each other through dozens of situations. Each knows what the other cares about, believes in, hopes for.

They're very genuinely in love. They're beginning to think marriage. There's still a lot of ground to cover before that happens, but it's not an unrealistic, purely fluffy dream either.

And one night they make love.

Cheap? Absolutely not. Just using each other? Absolutely not. So that makes it perfectly okay? No.

Doing something out of genuine love makes it *not cheap but not necessarily either right or smart.*

You can do a lot of things out of love that aren't right or smart. If someone harms or insults my wife, I can attack that person with a hatchet, and I may be doing it because I love my wife, but that doesn't make the action right, and it certainly doesn't make it smart. I might spend the rest of my life paying for something I did basically because I love her.

Two final observations on the "but if you love someone" consideration:

Love is not just a feeling. And, unfortunately, even *feeling in love* doesn't mean it's the real thing. You've seen that over and over, and maybe experienced it yourself.

Jack and Jill meet, feel the wonderful rush of first attraction, agree to go together, and everything looks and feels somewhere between terrific and perfect for two weeks, two months, maybe longer. But within a relatively short time, it's over. Maybe one of them finds out the other is actually kind of a jerk in spite of being cute. Maybe they just don't have much in common after all. Maybe…it could be anything. In any case, they end up, sometimes fairly soon, anywhere from being "just friends" to hating each other.

But for a while, remember, they were positive that this was absolute, real, genuine, lasting love.

Second, even if there's enough going in the relationship to call it love of some degree, how many times is this going to happen between early puberty and marriage? For many people, many times. That's okay. Most of us come together, split or drift apart, come together, split or drift apart with a number of people before we find the person we REALLY want and can spend the rest of our lives with.

If you buy the idea that any degree of love means having sex, you're going to end up pretty used by the time you find your actual marriage partner.

God really did have the right idea.

Difficult to live up to, no question about that. But the right idea.

Worth going for and living up to.

Which makes sense. This whole sex thing was God's idea.

CHAPTER TWENTY

. . . .

Sex III:
The !#ld%!m*n Crocodiles

" It's quiet out there."
"Yeah. TOO quiet."
—*Standard line from old movies right before an attack
by the other guys' army or an invasion force of nasty
but highly intelligent mutant mosquitoes, etc.*

Crocodiles. Yes, they're over there in Do-It Land, and they're real.

We're not going to spend a lot of time and space on this.

Every year there are more than one and a half million unplanned teen pregnancies, leading to the abortion-or-not decision and the keep-it-or-not decision. There are now more than twenty-five sexually transmitted diseases. (Rather recently there used to be far fewer than that; the Do-It-Anytime Revolution has spawned many more.)

If you want more statistics, they're not difficult to find. And they'll be out of date before too long, unless the country wakes up. We're tearing ourselves apart.

Bottom line: sex bites. That's it, there it is, tune it out if you want, but reality shows that sex can bite back.

Which is what makes people believe or want to believe the lie about safe sex, which is simply this: Take your pill or wear your condom and all is cool.

Bull.

There's a second syllable to that word; you can easily supply it. It fits.

The truth: The pill has at least a 6-percent failure rate even when used correctly (lots of sexually active women don't know how to use it), and it leads to thousands of medical complications, including death, every year. Depending on the study you read, the condom has a failure rate of somewhere between 8 and 25 percent. That's for the prevention of pregnancy, keeping a sperm cell from getting where the people involved don't want it to get. HIV, the AIDS virus, is 450 times *smaller* than a sperm cell. Consider the possibilities.

Safe sex is a lie.

But there's another lie behind the first one. It goes like this: No baby, no disease = no harm done. If you don't accidentally reproduce or get diseased reproductive equipment, everything's fine.

If that's true, then you're nothing more than a pair of ovaries and a vagina or a pair of testicles and a penis. "Safe sex" ignores every other part of you—the emotional, intellectual, spiritual—as though they didn't exist. Thousands upon thousands of people practice "safe sex" and end up with broken hearts, shattered, bleeding emotions, and a lousy feeling of being cheap and used.

That's a safe activity? Only if you're nothing more than your genitals. Because of the Do-It Revolution, we now have:

- Much more pain when the relationship breaks up, as (sorry, but you know this already anyway) *every one will do except the last one.*
- Far more pressure to do things that one partner—sometimes both—actually doesn't want to do.
- Far stronger tendency to see people simply or mainly as sex objects.
- Thousands upon thousands of babies and kids growing up without a father in their lives, sometimes never having seen or known their fathers—babies and kids who deserve a lot better than that.
- Fewer happy, permanent marriages.

- A decidedly cheapened, lesser meaning in making love.
- Worry about a date's past history and wondering if he or she is telling the truth about it.
- Worry about sexual performance ("Was I as good as his or her last partner?") instead of learning to make love with a spouse who loves you for you, not your performance.
- Skyrocketing, off-the-scale instances of date/acquaintance rape.
- Drastically increased concern and worry about whether someone truly loves you or is principally using you.
- Much heavier pressure to keep up a relationship that really isn't going anywhere except to bed.
- Mounds and piles of shattered dreams: college, career, hope for finding a true love—it could be a long list.
- Multiplying mountains of regret and sadness from something that was created to bring laughter, fulfillment, and joy.

Enough about crocodiles. Unfortunately, they're not just a bogeyman story. They're real.

Once again, God's directions come down to the same bottom line: God wants us to be happy with life, not have it bite back.

CHAPTER TWENTY-ONE

· · · · · · · · · · · · · · ·

Previews and Underwear

The following preview has been approved for all audiences:

"On a sudden journey from the only land they had ever known, they were absorbed into a world of light, a kingdom of glory, a realm of breathtaking beauty that would transform them forever!

"From the producer of Earth, the director of Life, and the award-winning animator of *RRRGHHRR IPP[P[[P][P* .... *TZZZ#PFTWURXIJGFPGLE%#LGGh wx^blecjhpfzz*.............. ....

"Ladies and gentlemen, we apologize. There seems to be a defect in this preview print."

Chances are that by now you've had the experience of wearing an extremely formal piece of clothing—a gown or a tux, complete with all the extras like matching shoes—to a formal occasion, like a wedding or a prom. Chances also are that you were (a) excited about how gorgeous, stunning, impressive, and so forth you looked in all this special clothing, and (b) extremely glad you didn't have to wear it for more than a few hours.

We're willing to put up with a little pinch here, a little restriction of movement there, for the sake of an occasion that isn't going to last more than a few hours. Besides, the beautiful but ill-fitting clothing isn't, well, *right next to us*. A cummerbund, for example, can make its presence felt very deeply when a guy has to bend over to retie shoes, for example, but it's not on his mind nonstop. Particularly not when he's dancing with a lovely girl.

Underwear is a different matter. (Pardon the comparison, but it's extremely accurate and clear.) You wear it all the time, not just on special occasions, and it *is* right next to you. If some part of it scratches or pinches or doesn't fit in general, it's not easy to tune out. A really bad fitting piece of underwear can sour your outlook on the world.

"Hey, Ken, how's it going?"

"Shut up."

"Man, what's your *problem?*"

"*Nothing!*" (Real answer: "I'm wearing my little brother's shorts by mistake.")

Again pardon the comparison, but in many ways, family and family relationships are like underwear: We take it for granted and often don't think about it much *until it begins to hurt* because family too *is right next to us.* We count on it to be there and be comfortable without our having to do any major adjusting. When we hurt because of it, everything is affected.

A year ago I had the most open, honest, trusting group of young people I've ever taught. They trusted one another with practically everything that was going on in their lives. No one broke the trust. We learned a lot together.

One of the things we learned is that family really matters. No matter how much young people want to be independent, to be on their own and "get away from all the rules," few things hurt as much as things gone wrong within the family. Even though we go outside our families in search of friendship and love, even though we try hard to matter to other people, the deepest pain comes from feeling that our families don't love us or that our lives don't matter to them.

Our instinct for good family relationships is built into us because family is built into life. God put it there. It's supposed to be a preview.

God fills life with neat things, and they're all messages, kind of like previews of an upcoming film called *Eternity.* Every genuinely good thing here on earth—roller coasters, pizza, hugs, Christmas trees, swimming pools, moonlight dances, and the great feeling of having done something good and right and helped someone—is God's way of saying, "Enjoy, but you haven't seen anything yet! Wait till you catch my next act. It's called Heaven." Home—family—is supposed to be a preview of heaven too, a place where you're accepted, supported, loved, and helped to grow.

But this is *earth*, not heaven. Christmas trees begin to droop, sometimes even topple over; days at the pool can bring sunburn; moonlight dances can end in heartbreak. And things go wrong at home.

Sometimes they seem bigger than they are, again because we expect a perfect, comfortable fit from something so close. When a mother loses her patience, it's easy to forget the countless meals she cooked and loads of laundry she did when she didn't feel like it, all the times she searched for missing shoes and boots and ball gloves. When a father loses his temper, it's easy to forget the times he fixed bicycles, drove to and from soccer practices and games, and worked when he didn't feel like it.

Sometimes things that go wrong *are* big. Parents may break up in a bitter, ugly divorce; even a "friendly" divorce isn't easy to take. A parent can become alcoholic or abusive. One parent may be completely or almost completely out of the picture. One of the saddest rising statistics is the number of teenage girls who skip the school's Father-Daughter Dance because there's no one to go there with or no one who wants to.

It's dumb to pretend these things don't hurt deeply, even though that's the most common reaction I hear: "...but it doesn't really bother me." That's nearly always a lie—not the evil kind of lie that attempts to hurt and deceive, but the self-defense kind of lie that tries to build a wall of denial to keep pain out.

Suffering in general provides one of the biggest temptations to give up on God. Every one of us has heard and probably also said, "How can God let something like that happen?" Suffering in and because of family may top the list.

It's okay to be angry, even at God, when the world in your household is or seems to be falling apart or blowing up. What's not okay is to take it out on everyone around you, and giving up in general, including on God.

In a strange way, even the hurt can be a message from God: "I couldn't keep this from happening because I decided to make and let people be free. But you can decide to keep it from happening in the home, the family, that *you* build."

Even then, it's neither right nor healthy to spend most of the time tossing accusations at those people who couldn't make home work out really well, even though they may have tried pretty hard.

Spend some time thinking about what's *right* with your home and family. Chances are there's an awful lot more than you're usually aware of, just as you probably have far more good-underwear days than you usually think about.

And remember that all the good things are a preview. Don't give up on *Eternity* and its Producer just because the previews are limited.

. . . .

CHAPTER TWENTY-TWO

Metamorphosis!! ("Look It Up.")

"**W**ho are YOU?" Andy asked the strange creature who had appeared out of nowhere.

"Grizzelda Drainworthy, Zapper Second Class. A zapper."

"A zapper?"

"That's what we're called in the trade. To you folks, we're known as fairy godmothers, wizards, that sort of thing. I can turn you into almost anything but an intergalactic overlord or an ancient pharaoh. For that, you need a zapper first class."

"I don't get it."

"You know, *ZAP* and you're changed. The frog becomes a handsome prince, Cinderella gets a total makeover. Surely you've read the stories. What would you like? I do a *great* Cinderella thing, by the way."

"Hey, I'm a guy!"

"Oh, right, SORRY. How about a TV wrestler?"

Once upon a time there was a young man and a young woman. They met at a mixer after a football game. They liked each other, started going together, fell in love, got engaged, and finally were married.

For a while they were real, regular people, living in the real world. They knew what life was all about and how to enjoy it. They were, in fact, moderately and sometimes maximally cool. Then, one day, they got zapped and all that changed: *They got turned into parents!*

Suddenly, they stopped living in the real world. They began worrying about dumb things like cutting the grass and keeping the house in order and not spending too much money. It was truly sad: sometimes they even counted calories and fat grams. The fun of staying up late and turning the music up loud got erased from their memory banks.

"Don't you ever want to have fun?" a member of their household asked the mother once.

"Why of course, dear," the mother answered as she looked up from the latest issue of *Sewing Rooms Illustrated*. "Why, I'm having just tons and oodles of fun right now."

Okay, that's an exaggeration. But it comes close to the way young people sometimes see their parents. Children often wish they could zap their parents back into "real" people with a "real" life. The problem is, what's "real"? People tend to define "real" as "just like or pretty much like me."

Many things make one person different from another. Growing up is just one of them. You've passed the stage of playing with dolls or sneaking pet frogs into the house. But there was a time when those things were the "real" world, the important world, to you.

In the years to come, each stage will seem as if "*This* is what it's all about" while you're there. Even in areas in which you stay somewhat the same, the world around you will change. Strange but true: there will come a day when you're playing the tapes or CDs you grew up with—*the* really great all-time best-ever music—and your kids will say, "How can you *stand* that old stuff!!??"

It shouldn't be surprising that parents are different from you. It's not always easy to handle, but you probably wouldn't want it any other way. Picture it: you come home and find Mom practicing cheerleading in the middle of the kitchen, waving pompoms and chewing bubblegum. Are you overjoyed that she's turned back into a "real" person, or are you a little worried about her? You dash into the bathroom and catch Dad standing in front of the mirror, flexing and checking to see if his pecs and abs are tanned and cut well enough. Would you think he's returned to reality or sliding into fantasy?

We have to accept one another as real people, being real where we are in life. Parents are real people trying to do a pretty tough job.

Think of something you've been in charge of and responsible for: party plans, dance decorations, car wash, canoe trip, service outreach, anything. You wanted it to be right, even though it wouldn't last forever. Think of the feelings you had at each stage: starting out with enthusiasm and hoping for the very best; getting a little worried when things didn't work out the way they should have, but picking up the pieces and making a fresh start; getting a little tired—not upset and disgusted, just simply tired—of having to be on the job when you'd like some time to yourself.

Now take those same feelings and imagine that this time you're in charge of a human being—a person who *will* last forever. And imagine (shouldn't be difficult) that you care deeply about that person.

Enough that sometimes you say, "Absolutely not" when it would be so easy to be the cool hero and say, "Sure, go ahead, just kind of be careful."

Even families with goodwill dripping down the kitchen wall will experience parent–teen conflicts. You can pave a smoother road toward resolving them by remembering that there's a difference between genuinely wanting to get along better and simply wanting to win the argument or the war. If you (or a parent) talk only with a view of making the other person say, "I've been *so terribly, totally wrong!* I feel just awful!" that's just wanting to conquer, and it nearly always guarantees that everybody will lose.

It also helps a lot to talk about events and feelings; that's very different from making broad accusations.

For example: "When I tried to tell you how much this party means to me, you just yelled and walked away. That made me feel like my feelings don't even matter, and that hurts." That's a legitimate statement, and it has a much better chance at getting a good reception, even if the party still gets a "no."

"You *never* understand me. You never understand *anything!* You don't even *care!*" THAT is 1,000-percent, guaranteed, pure emotional poison. Why? It's actually a vicious accusation that just can't be completely true, and making it amounts to a personal attack. The other person goes into fight-back mode against the accusation, and the issue that brought the conflict or misunderstanding gets sidetracked, then lost (sometimes almost forgotten!), and stays unsettled.

One day the metamorphosis (if you didn't know, you looked it up, right?) will probably happen to you. Only it won't feel like a sudden metamorphosis. It'll feel pretty much just like being you, except that now, being a parent, you're responsible for a human being.

Which is the most awesome thing you'll ever do: making another human being. Anything else you do or make or put together, whether it's a bicycle, an Olympic record, or an international business empire, will eventually crumble and die.

But not your kids. Your kids, just as you, will live forever. You'll want their lives to turn out right and happy. And sometimes you'll risk appearing "unreal" to help make that happen.

CHAPTER TWENTY-THREE

CHAPTER TWENTY-THREE

. . . .

2 Minus 1 and Other Differences

"What are those bumpy things in the water?"

"Those are called ripples, Honey. You made them when you tossed the stone in the water."

"Where do they go?"

"They just go out and out."

"Do they hit anything?"

"Well, sort of. See that little twig in the water? The ripples are making it bounce up and down, see? Ripples can make lots of things happen."

You and a friend are standing in line at a deli, okay? Behind the counter is a nice lady who would like to take your friend's order, but it's not working out too well. Your friend stands there mumbling over and over, "Should I get the baked ham, salami, and Limburger with tomato and hot relish on rye...or should I maybe get the smoked ham, pepperoni, and sharp cheddar with onion, mayo, olives, and green pepper on a wheat bun...or maybe the garlic bologna, smoked pork, and...."

Your friend needs help. You need to step in and say, "*What's the difference?* You're going to get heartburn anyway, so stop holding up the line."

Good old "What's the difference?"

It's an attitude, an outlook, and sometimes we need it, or we need to hear it from someone, as in the situation above. It helps us recognize small stuff that we really need to see as small stuff because it *is.*

79

But if we get used to using it as an outlook for everything, it can make big stuff *seem* like small stuff, and that's dangerous. Don't let an all-the-time "What's the difference?" outlook rub off on you. It can turn people into killers.

We'll invent a fictional character. Call him Deke.

In ninth grade, one of his favorite pastimes was making life hell for Mr. Winter, his history teacher. It was Winter's first year of teaching; he wasn't a pro at handling a class yet; he was easy to manipulate. Sometimes Deke even organized his friends to do the same genuinely mean things to Winter that he did. After all, he explained, what difference did it make? Winter got paid anyway whether he was in control of the class or not, and besides, somebody had to toughen him up.

One of Deke's main weekend things was putting away most of a twelve-pack. Everybody drinks now and then, loosens up, gets crazy, he said. And besides, what was the difference? He'd been putting away a few cans here and there since junior high, and he wasn't rotting away in some rehab unit. That's what he kept telling his friend Larry, who wasn't much of a drinker until Deke really pressured him with something about being a real guy instead of a little altar boy. So Larry got royally fried one Friday, decided he liked it, and did it again a couple weeks later.

In junior year, Deke was going with Carrie. He convinced her that (a) he really liked her, and (b) everybody was doing it because this was the '90s, for God's sake, and that's what people do when they like each other. If you're married, fine; if you're not, fine, what's the difference? So they had sex quite a few times. Carrie really wanted to stop, so Deke soon dropped her and spread some graphic stories about how easy she was to get to. He didn't miss her all that much because, as he explained to a friend, what difference did it make? There were lots of girls.

Deke is in his senior year of college now. He hasn't made the dean's list, and he won't be at the awards ceremony, but he's not down the tube, either. He doesn't see many people from his high school, but he doesn't regret anything from those years either. After all, what difference does it make now?

Actually, a good bit.

It made a difference to Mr. Winter. He's not teaching anymore. That first year was enough to shake his confidence and make him decide that the neat things he wanted to do in teaching just weren't worth getting a nervous breakdown over. He's working at a job he doesn't really like, but at least there aren't people deliberately trying to make his life miserable. With a little more experience, he would have been a great teacher. He would have helped a lot of young people because he's an exceptionally understanding person. If only his first year hadn't been such a rotten encounter.

It made a difference to Larry. Larry was one of those people with a body chemistry that gets hooked awfully easily. Deke still drinks too much now and then, although he's not a confirmed alcoholic. But Larry is. He washed out of college in his first year. Bounces around in entry-level jobs, never holding one for very long.

It made a difference to Carrie. The experience with Deke left her feeling pretty used, and Deke's stories made her sound pretty usable to other guys like him. One of them told her some of the same things Deke did. Carrie hoped that *this* time it was true and it *would* be love. She now has a kid, three years old, whom she dearly loves but can't really care for the way she'd like to. The father of the kid is in the navy. Carrie is actually glad of that; she doesn't want to see him.

It made a difference to Sarah, too. That's Carrie's child. Sarah is starting to wish she had someone to call "Daddy."

Every now and then, just for a moment or so, Deke thinks about the people he used to know in high school and wonders what they're up to these days. But he doesn't make any effort to find out. After all, that was then and this is now, and what difference would it make?

CHAPTER TWENTY-FOUR

. . . .

Rational Ice for
Seventh-Commandment Pain

"Looks like you've got a broken ankle."

"Hurts pretty much."

"Well, you don't want to live with a lot of pain. Here, take this."

"What is it?"

"A painkiller. Pretty strong, really works. Keep taking them."

"What else should I do?"

"Nothing. You'll still be a kid with a broken ankle, but you won't *feel* that way."

"Youth Returns Lost Billfold and $700."

"Woman Finds Diamond Ring Worth Thousands Hands It Over."

"Man Returns Dropped Deposit Bag, $15,000."

Every now and then you see headlines like these. What's your reaction? Here are some possibilities:

"Those people are stupid for not keeping the stuff. Who would ever find out? If somebody's dumb enough to lose a billfold or a diamond or a bank deposit, they deserve to lose it. I'd keep it and not tell anybody."

"They did the right thing, the only thing you *can* do if you have a conscience. If something doesn't belong to you, you don't take it; and if you find it, you try to get it back to whoever owns it. Simple as that."

You can tell that those positions are opposites. Here are some in-between, trying-to-have-it-both-ways positions:

"With the billfold, I'd keep the money, because after all you deserve a reward, but I wouldn't use the credit cards or anything, and I'd send the billfold back so they wouldn't have to get a new driver's license and stuff."

"Anybody who has a diamond ring can afford to lose it. They'll just get another one. So I'd sell the ring but like maybe give some of the money to the poor or something."

"I think everything happens for a purpose, so I'd figure that finding something like that was meant to be. I wouldn't use the money for stupid stuff, but I'd pay all my bills and everything."

Some people would bring in an "it all depends" clause of some kind: "It all depends: like if your family was starving, or your kid needed medicine you couldn't afford."

Sure, extreme conditions like that can change a situation, but it's hardly worth the time to consider a case that isn't likely to happen. We're talking about regular old ordinary life. And in that case, it *would* depend on something: on whether or not the person who finds the lost articles is a thief.

"Thief" is an ugly word. It suggests a lowlife; nobody likes it spoken about him or her.

But we live in a culture that idolizes having and owning nice, often glitzy things, and the more the better. The pressure to get more of these things can be heavy, and that creates the temptation to get them whether we have the money to buy them or not. And *that,* plus not wanting to look or feel like a common thief, creates the need to "rationalize" taking or keeping things that don't belong to us. "Rationalizing," we mentioned earlier, is the technique of inventing phony reasons to feel better about doing something that we know very well is wrong. Unfortunately, it's easy to get very good at it.

Here are four of the most common ways to rationalize stealing, whether that's deliberately taking something or keeping a found item that obviously belongs to someone else and whose rightful owner could, at least probably, be found.

1. *It actually belongs to me anyway.*

   Example: "You know, when you think about it, this store rips customers off all the time. Look at the prices around here—they're terrible. This store probably makes 1,000-percent profit on all this stuff. And with all the things I've bought here in the past, I've probably paid a couple hundred dollars more than I should have if their prices were fair. So actually *they owe me*. So if I sort of take this camera with me when I leave, it's not really stealing. I'm just taking part of what they owe me."

2. *I need/deserve it more than they do.*

   Example: "What does Sheila do to earn all that money she always has? Like this twenty she left lying here in her locker. Not a blasted thing. Her parents are loaded and just give it to her. Me, I work like crazy for minimum, and I have to buy most of my clothes. It's not fair. If things were fair, this twenty would belong to me for all the work I do, instead of being part of Sheila's small change. So if I take it, I'm just making things a little more fair, the way they should be."

3. *They deserve to lose this.*

   Example (continued): "Sheila is *such* a snob. Always flaunting what she buys and does and gets with all the money she has. She's really obnoxious about it a lot of the time. If something makes a person obnoxious, they deserve to lose some of it. Sheila deserves to lose this twenty. Besides, she shouldn't be leaving money around like this. That's careless. If I take it, it'll teach her a lesson to be more careful. So, actually, taking it is probably a *good* thing."

4. *Nobody's going to get hurt.*

   Example: "People in this part of town have money dripping out their ears. They're filthy rich. So what does it matter if I rip off this kid's ten-speed? The kid won't get hurt; Mom and Dad will just go right out and buy a brand-new one, probably an even better one than this. So, actually, I'm doing the kid a favor. And on top of that, the people themselves won't have to pay for it. Their insurance will. Everybody's got insurance for stuff that disappears. So nobody's getting hurt, and that means it's not wrong."

All these excuses have something in common: They help thieves not to feel so much like thieves.

. . . .

CHAPTER TWENTY-FIVE

To Beat or Not to Beat the System

*"*All you need to do is put your signature right here. Here, you can use this pen, and this document will give you sole rights to collect tolls from all vehicles on the Golden Gate Bridge. Hire some people to work different shifts, all day and night. You won't have to pay them much, and you'll have your $250,000 back in less than six months. Pretty good deal, don't you think?"

"Well, I hope so. This is my life's savings, you know. Are you sure I can trust you?"

"Hey, did Napoleon take over in 1799 or not?"

"What does Napoleon have to do with it?"

"Trust me, there's a connection."

P. T. Barnum was a circus owner way back in the days when the only person who was thinking about you was God. Barnum's circus was one of the three that merged and became the big circus we know today as Ringling Brothers, Barnum and Bailey.

According to an often-told story, Barnum once had a problem in the tent that housed his wild-animal display. Many people had never seen wild animals before, sometimes not even in pictures, so they stood there fascinated and wouldn't leave. (Remember, this was back in the days before National Geographic specials.)

Soon the tent became congested, and people who were standing outside waiting to pay and go in got tired and went away. Anything that cut into profits was very upsetting to P. T. Barnum. But he couldn't exactly force people out of the tent. He had to find a way to get them to leave.

He did.

He had noticed that people seemed to think the female of a species was wilder and fiercer than the male. So his wild animals were the lioness, the tigress, the leopardess, and so forth. He put up a sign above a small corridor in the tent: "This way to the Egress!"

An *egress!* In a display all its own. It must be the meanest, fiercest, wildest animal of all! That's what many people thought anyway, and that's what P. T. Barnum wanted them to think. They followed the sign and found themselves outside.

An egress is another name for an exit.

Nobody marched Barnum down to municipal court and charged him with fraud. The charge probably would not have stuck anyway; the sign told the perfect truth.

"Fraud" exists all around us, although it sounds like a strictly adult thing, something the FBI investigates. And as for cases that come to court, it *is* an adult thing. Kids seldom try to sell Pennsylvania residents an acre of "all-natural Florida real estate" that turns out to be swampland inhabited by water snakes and a few billion tons of algae. But the adults who do get convicted of things like that may have gotten their start much earlier in life.

Like in a middle-grades math class or high-school biology class. It can begin with cheating on tests, book reports, projects, term papers, almost anything that goes on in school. That's a type of fraud because anything a student does is supposed to reflect what he or she actually knows, actually has done, and has genuinely earned.

Can you beat the system and get away with it? Can you come out looking fairly academically cool even though you didn't do or learn much? Depends on the teacher; you know that, and so do I. Some can smell cheating techniques that are just starting to form in a student's brain, while others seem to be floating around in some other dimension while practically out-in-the-open cheating happens right in front of them.

To cheat or not to cheat. It all depends on how real you want to be. We each got a certain unique combination of abilities of various kinds and the instructions from God, "Go out and make me proud of you." What you do with that ability is up to you. You can work with it and be genuinely proud of what you genuinely accomplish, or you can try to beat the system and get results that merely *look* as if they're yours.

There will always be an endless supply of reasons why it's "okay *this time*": The test is totally unfair. The questions are too difficult. The classes didn't prepare for the test. The material is stupid; nobody needs to know this stuff. There wasn't enough time to study. A bad grade will make Mom and Dad even more upset when they're already upset about other things, and would put a lot of strain on the whole family.

And there will always be two main excuses to make it seem okay *anytime*. They're the same two tired, old, worn-out, rubbed-ragged excuses that are used for almost everything but attacking other life forms on distant planets: Everybody does it, and nobody gets hurt.

The majority of people *don't* cheat. That's the fact and the truth. The people who refuse to cheat, even when it would be relatively easy to get away with, are not strange creatures who don't live in the real world. Being real, in fact, is exactly what they're doing.

As for nobody's getting hurt, it sometimes looks as if that's the case at the time. Jack sneaks a sideways glance at Jill's history test, notices that Jill feels Napoleon seized power in France in 1799, and puts the same thing on his test paper. Darned if that wasn't exactly the year Napoleon did it. Score a correct answer for both of them. Where's the problem? Who's getting hurt?

It goes beyond the initial actual lie (Jack is saying, "I knew this" when he didn't). It enters the pool of times when Jack beat the system. When he does that often enough, beat-the-system becomes a way of looking at life wherever it can be made to work.

It's fifteen years later, and Jack is now co-owner of a construction company. He's still finding a way to beat the system and make some extra bucks.

When people buy one of his new homes, do they crawl up and

around in it to check that all the insulation is there that's supposed to be? Of course not. Do the buyers stand and watch the driveway being poured to see if the grade of concrete is okay or substandard? Of course not.

The only person who's going to know is the building inspector, and she's a friend of Jack's, especially since they split the bucks saved by cutting corners.

But then one day a worker gets fed up and blows the whistle, or somehow somebody *does* find out. The newspaper investigates further and prints a big report. Nobody, obviously, wants to buy a home from that company now, so it folds and quickly goes out of business. Jack is out of a job; the building inspector is fired.

They got what they deserved, right? Yes.

But they're not the only ones involved. *Everybody* at the company is out of a job, including honest people who need a job. *Every worker's family* is involved.

Jack's wife and kids are involved.

The incident unleashes a lot of letters to the newspaper about corruption in government and how it's about time for decent citizens and taxpayers to put their foot down until people in government clean up their shop. As a result, a tax levy that is genuinely needed to improve schools gets voted down, and thousands of kids work without things that would have given them a better education.

Nobody got hurt back when a piece of Napoleon information got lifted from one paper to another? Not exactly. Along with other instances, it helped get the ball ("beat the system") rolling. It just took a few years for the ball to hit a lot of people.

The above is a fictional example, but it certainly isn't impossible or even unlikely. It's not difficult to imagine stories like that being played out all the time, and you don't want to be a part of them. You're better than that.

The real you and the real accomplishments you really achieve—that's the real world.

CHAPTER TWENTY-SIX
• • • • • • • • • • • • •
Club Membership

"**A**re you a member here?"

"Gosh, I sure hope so. I thought I was. Actually, I'm sure I am."

"Well, I'm sure you are, too. Step over here to the pneumascope, just in case anybody ever questions it, and…well, there it is, clear as crystal: made in the image and likeness of God, definitely. Sorry there was any question. Go right ahead and take part in anything we have going here, with full rights and privileges, and please enjoy your stay with us. We'd also appreciate anything you can share with us or teach us. Each person made in the image of God is made just a little differently, and it's to everyone's benefit to learn from one another."

If only it were that easy, and actually, it should be.

If somebody showed us how to read others' thoughts, probably the first thing we'd do is psych out what others really think of us. Not everybody is up front with his or her complete thoughts and feelings, especially about other people. People might think, "The way you act is seriously stupid sometimes," but they're not comfortable saying so; or they might think, "You're really special and wonderful," but they're too shy to say so.

If we accidentally get the chance to secretly overhear other people talking about us, we listen with even better attention than we did when we first overheard people talking about sex. Picture these two imaginary situations:

First, let's say your name is Bill Thompson. You come back into the school building a half hour or so after dismissal to get a notebook that you forgot. Right before you enter the classroom, you hear voices from inside and quickly realize that it's a group of teachers talking about you.

"Thompson's a good choice for the citizenship award, don't you think?"

"Decent choice, I guess, but I don't know if we should go with him."

"Why not?"

"Well, there's publicity and pictures. Thompson's not the greatest-looking kid, you know. I mean, he's not Quasimodo, but he doesn't have a fresh, clean-cut look. The school's image is a factor here too, you know."

"Good point. Is he athletic?"

"Another minus. Played a little reserve basketball one year, but he wasn't that good. It makes a better impression on the public if you've got a kid who's a good citizen and a jock at the same time."

"True. What's his father do?"

"Dunno. Doesn't live with him; the family's divorced."

"Well, that ices it. We need a kid from a traditional family. It makes a good photo in the paper when you have a smiling parent on each side of the kid."

Now let's say your name is Lisa and you're going with a guy named Matt. You also stop outside the classroom door because inside the room Matt and a friend are talking about you.

"You still going with Lisa?"

"Yeah, for a while, but it's about time for a change. I mean, she's all right, but she's not exactly a goddess."

"Really. Great legs, though."

"Yeah, fantastic legs, but the rest is a little too ordinary."

"Who are you going to get next?"

"Shelley. Now *there* is a goddess. It might take a couple more weeks. Some chicks you gotta work on gradually."

"When are you going to dump Lisa?"

"Soon as Shelley says she'll go with me. But till then I gotta have somebody for the weekend."

If you're Lisa or Bill, there's hardly a word for how you feel. "Angry" doesn't come close, and even "furious" sounds weak. Above all, you're incredibly, deeply hurt.

The adults are talking about Bill Thompson and kids in general as though they were things, not persons. Bill's worth as a person and his worthiness for the award don't really matter. What matters is that the school have an exhibit, the "right" kind of trophy to impress the public.

Matt and his friend are talking about Lisa and girls in general in the same way, as *objects* to be used. Lisa isn't a girl; she's a body. She isn't a friend; she's a piece of property. She's about to be tossed out like an old concert jersey is when a newer, supposedly cooler group makes it to the top of the charts.

What makes these situations so painful is also what makes them so very wrong: people are being talked about, treated, and used as though they were things.

Unfortunately, it's really easy to see people that way. There are, after all, so many of them.

If you found a diamond out of a million pebbles in the backyard, you'd either treasure it or recognize its worth and sell it for a great deal of money. Why? There aren't that many diamonds. That's what makes it valuable. But if every yard was littered with millions of diamonds, they'd seem ordinary. In fact, they would *be* ordinary, not particularly valuable at all.

But it doesn't work that way with people. The fact that there are millions of them walking around the planet doesn't lessen the value of each single one. Each person is just as valuable as if he or she were the *only* one because each is created in the image of God, and that just plain settles it.

How can we tell if we're respecting others as persons instead of using them as objects? Jesus gave us an excellent guideline. It's foolproof, actually:

In everything do to others as you would have them do to you. (Matthew 7:12)

· · · · · · · · · · · · · · · ·

CHAPTER TWENTY-SEVEN

Getting Sucked into the War Machine

"Oh, how wonderful! It's been too long since we've had a delightful little war. Almost a month, I think."

"Your Highness, I'm not sure it's wise to engage in war at this particular moment."

"Why not? We can't put up with this kind of insult, and you know how I love to plan a war."

"Yes, Your Highness, but several strategic forces are still recovering from the previous war. Further strain on them at this point may not be wise."

"Which strategic forces?"

"Well, there's your blood pressure, your grade-point average, your general emotional health, your...."

Kathy is having a party Saturday night. Maybe a dozen to sixteen people, something like that. A regular party.

Usually, Julie would be invited. Julie is one of Kathy's close friends—no, she *used to be* a close friend. But Julie deliberately isn't invited to this party, even though she's the *reason* for the party.

What happened? Something Julie said. Actually, Kathy didn't hear it herself, but Gail and Debbie *said* that Julie said it, and that was enough. When Kathy thinks people are out to get her, she doesn't need much in the way of concrete evidence. The truth is, she loves a war. It almost seems as though she's not happy unless there's a campaign going against somebody or other.

She hadn't been planning a party at all until this happened. She can't really afford it right now. To finance the party, she'll have to use a good chunk of new-clothes money she was saving up. But the party seems like a good way to get back at Julie. First, there will be the fact that Julie isn't invited. Second, Kathy will put pressure on some of Julie's more easily led friends and make sure that they come, so it will look as though they've decided that their loyalties lie with Kathy, not Julie.

(There just may be a few people at this point thinking, "How incredibly immature" and "That's girls for you." Point number one is true, obviously, but point number two is completely off target. The same things happen with guys; they just go about it a little differently.)

In any case, what we're concerned with here is not Kathy's less-than-mature plans or even how this whole thing got started and what, if any, truth is behind it. What's at stake here is Julie's reaction. Let's look at a couple of ways she can go. Call them Plan A and Plan B—which won't win any awards for imaginative titling, but they're easy to keep straight.

Plan A

Julie hears from her friend Mary that Kathy has suddenly planned a party and doesn't intend to invite "that witch Julie." "*She's* the witch!" Mary hisses.

"'Witch' is too nice for her," Julie mutters between clenched teeth. "She is going to be *so* sorry!"

It's fourth bell, lunch. Julie has a big Spanish test coming up next bell, and she was planning to spend some time during lunch on last-minute review because she really needs a good grade on this test. But she can't think about that now; there's something else far more important: she has to find out exactly who's been invited to Kathy's party. Then, when she finds out, she has to see if they've said they would go, or what the status is, and above all try to talk them out of going if they're not sure what they're going to do.

Three names come to mind as people who would probably be more loyal to her than to Kathy: Traci, Ann, and Kim. She maybe has time to track them down and still eat a little lunch.

She succeeds with Traci and for a couple minutes feels a little better, a little sense of victory.

But Ann says, "Well, I guess if you're invited to a party, you should go unless you *really* don't want to or something. I mean, I'm sorry you weren't invited, but I can't do anything about that." Julie immediately labels Ann an official (and brand-new) enemy along with Kathy. Now she has two people to get back at.

She can't find Kim. She spends a lot of time in wondering where Kim stands on this party issue and trying to think up things to say that will really put the pressure on Kim to boycott the party. There's enough acid in her gut (and heart and mind and on her tongue) to give several gallons of Maalox and Mylanta a real battle.

Consequently, she blows the Spanish test. She doesn't even have time to finish it because she spends a minute here and two minutes there rehearsing exactly what she'll say and do the next time she meets Kathy.

During last bell, she writes a note to give Jan to give to Kim on the bus. It's about Kathy, very little of it based on fact, and filled with language and references you wouldn't want your grandmother to even know that you know. But a teacher sees the note being passed and intercepts it; in the emotion of the moment, Julie smart-mouths back and gets detention.

This drives her crazy. It's not just the detention; she can handle that. It's the fact that *today* it's a waste of extremely valuable time that she needs to call a half dozen people, trying to figure out who's on her side, who's on Kathy's side, who's in the middle, who's going to the party for sure, who's not, who doesn't know, who heard what from whom about what and whom....

Her life has become a battleground full of allies and enemies, attack positions and defenses and weapons, fear and doubt, tension and hate.

Plan B

Julie hears from her friend Mary that Kathy has suddenly planned a party and doesn't intend to invite "that witch Julie." "*She's* the witch!" Mary hisses.

"She's just mad and acting really stupid," Julie says. "She's trying to get back at me, but there's really nothing for her to get back about. I didn't say anything about her."

"What are you going to do about it?" Mary asks.

"Why should I *do* anything about it?" Julie asks. "She'll get over it. We've been mad at each other before. She's just going to an awful lot of trouble to fight over it this time."

"Aren't you *hurt?*"

"*Sure.* But I'm not going to ruin my life over it. I can't go to a party Saturday anyway; I have to babysit."

"You mean you're *not going to do anything?*" Mary is having a hard time with Julie's reaction.

"Sure. I'm going to forgive her and get on with my life."

Compare the results of each plan. In particular, compare the results within Julie, the effects on her life.

Jesus, a.k.a. the Prince of Peace, knew what he was talking about when he recommended forgiveness.

CHAPTER TWENTY-EIGHT
. . . .

UFOs and
Seven-Year-Old Warriors

"Do you believe in aliens and UFOs?"

"I dunno. Don't think about it much. Doesn't really matter to me as long as they don't mess up my date with..."

"Well, they're HERE!"

"Sure."

"No, REALLY! But they're not from outer space. They live IN-SIDE the earth! It's hollow. That's why scientists and the air force can't find them! There's this opening into the earth at the North Pole. That's where their 'spaceships' come from and go back to!"

"Did you have pizza with extra anchovies again?"

"No, REALLY, it's all in this book I just read!"

We take you now to one of those places on the planet where violent confrontations are, unfortunately, an almost daily occurrence: a second-grade playground. Let's listen.

"You're a jerk!"

"You're a *double* jerk!"

"I ain't scared of you!"

"You *better* be scared 'cause I can beat you up *bad!*"

"I can beat you up *badder.*"

Who are these two? A couple of kids about, oh, seven years old. Listen carefully as the plot thickens, and for heaven's sake don't laugh.

"You couldn't beat up an ant!"

"Yeah, I could. I could beat up an ape! You couldn't beat up a lightning bug!"

"I could beat up a *tiger,* and I can beat *you* up just like [insert name of current Saturday-morning cartoon superhero]!"

"I can beat *you* up just like Arnell Shortzegger!" [*Hush.* I told you *not to laugh.*]

It's time. Kid A makes a couple of fists and moves toward Kid B. Kid B backs off a half step and circles around. This gives Kid A some confidence; he moves in with hands revolving like an off-center windmill. Kid B protects his head with forearms and decides to attack from below; he kicks. He looks like he's practicing the Charleston or trying out for a chorus line.

What caused this Battle of the Titans? Serious stuff. Kid A accused Kid B of having big ears, so Kid B made a remark about Kid A's runny nose.

Your reactions, please.

If only those two little kids knew how dumb they look trying to act like professional fighting machines. If only they knew how stupid the whole thing *is!* Stupid, dumb, silly, pointless, and wrong.

Easy to see when you're watching seven-year-olds.

So why will the same thing seem (to some people) reasonable, worthwhile, even dramatic and admirable when they get older?

Let's add seven to ten years or so to our pair of kids. The confrontation won't be over big ears and runny noses anymore. It's more likely to be a girlfriend or simply a matter of reputation. The point is, though, that now they're capable of doing serious physical damage to each other.

Add weapons, and they're capable of permanently wrecking each other's lives and even killing each other. It happens. You know that.

It's just as stupid, just as pointless, but even far more wrong now that they're older. Violence is opposed to everything Jesus taught; it's as un-Christian as human behavior can get.

There's a distinction between violence and needed force. If you break up a fight (whether you're being attacked or someone else is) by pinning the attacker on the ground and putting his arms in a hammerlock until he decides that fighting wasn't such a cool idea after all, that's one thing. Call it force. Just enough force to stop the aggressive action, no more. Fine.

But if you go further and bloody his face (or later wreck some property), that's violence, and it's absolutely dead wrong.

The world is already in pain; read the sad headlines. We Christians above all can't add to it. We can't get caught up in it or admire and applaud it when it's going on around us.

Somewhere, probably from many sources, the idea has spread that to be really tough, cool, independent, and important you have to make people hurt, at least now and then. You put them down, make them afraid of you, mess with their feelings and their lives. You walk through life like a piece of living artillery calling the shots, getting your way, leaving hurt feelings spread along the path behind you. Loving and caring are weakness; shoving people around is strength.

Even the idea of alien beings driving UFOs in and out of the North Pole makes more sense than that.

Cruelty shows weakness. Love and caring are the signs of strength.

· · · · · · · · · · · · · · ·

CHAPTER TWENTY-NINE

Yes, You're One of *Them!*

"Francis? Saint Francis of Assisi, I mean. Are you tuned in up there?"

"Of course. Tell your daughter she has one of the cutest cats ever. I love animals, you know."

"I know. About this book I'm writing for young people—do you mind if I put them in a group with you?"

"Mind? PLEASE don't put them anywhere else!"

"Okay, thanks. Now put me on with Joan of Arc. Is she there?"

"She's right here. Here, Joan, it's for you."

"Joan here."

"Hi, Joan, this is Jim. Do you mind if I put the young people I'm writing for in the same…"

"Do I mind if you call them saints or saints in the making? Didn't mean to interrupt, but I like cutting to the bottom line; goes with the liberated-lady thing, I guess. Listen, if you DON'T do that, you and I will have a serious talk when you get up here. We all feel that way."

"Okay. Actually, I was pretty sure. But thanks for making it clear."

This is about your being holy, *and I don't want to hear any static* (there are other words, but we'd better use "static") *about it*. People in general have some major problems and attitudes about holiness; young people in particular have problems with it. Sorry; it's true. Here are a few:

- It's great for saints. That's not me. I'm just not that type. (I'm normal.)
- If I ever *do* get holy, it'll be when I'm too old or too weird to do anything else. Like have fun.
- I tried it when I was little. It wore off or something, or probably I just wasn't any good at it.
- Great idea if you have time. But I've got soccer practice after school and a research paper due the day after tomorrow.
- Just when I think I might be slightly into it, I do something not-so-great that proves I'm not.

Imagine people who belong to a club, a special organization. They've got their official membership cards in their billfolds or purses or somewhere, but they look at the membership cards and don't believe that their names are actually supposed to be printed there, as though they were looking at a fake ID. Or they keep trying to *hide* the membership cards and pretend they don't really own them. Or they carry the cards, but they're scared to death of *using* them! Or they use the membership cards now and then (sometimes more often than they realize) but don't count themselves as real members because they don't check into every possible activity every day.

Holiness is like that something we often don't or won't look at; or that we have trouble admitting, even to ourselves, that we possess in any way; or that we're scared to death of pursuing and raising ourselves to further levels of participation.

But I've taught an awful lot of holy kids, whether they believed they were or not. Most of them probably didn't. If you walked into my classroom and saw them, you wouldn't step back and think, "Wowww, *saints!*" But they were. I could fill another book with their stories.

What do we think holiness is, anyway? Becoming some unreal being who floats around in an unreal world? Or living in some other world most of the time and coming down to the real world now and then to preach the gospel?

True, many saints boarded ships headed for distant lands and talked about Jesus to people there who had never heard of him.

True, many saints got their heads chopped off or were thrown off cliffs or were burned to death because they wouldn't say that Jesus was a fantasy or a fake.

True, many saints spent their lives out of the mainstream of "regular life," just kind of hanging out with the Lord and praying for others because that's what they were called to do.

All those saints were wonderfully holy and spiritually cool and anything similar you want to say about them. They're our heroes, or should be. But our problem is thinking we have to be exactly like them in every detail because, apparently, that's what holiness "is." Our problem is thinking that if we can't duplicate most of the activities and details of *their* lives, then we're just not the "type" to be holy.

But the bottom line is simply this: holiness comes down to *doing the best job we can in the work God has called us to do at whatever point we are in our lives.*

Maybe that *is* going to a foreign land and preaching the good news of Jesus to people who have never heard of him. Maybe it's serving vegetable soup at an inner-city center for the alcoholic or homeless, and trying to spread a ray of hope.

Maybe it's being the best, most honest, most conscientious construction worker, investment counselor, nurse, mechanic, restaurant manager, professional athlete, mail carrier, law-enforcement officer, real-estate agent, or electrician you can be, along with the best wife/mother or husband/father you can be.

It comes down to slugging it out the best you can, in the way Jesus would want you to live, in whatever circumstances you find yourself. Maybe that means being open to having a vision from heaven (which has to be kind of a scary thing to handle, at least at first), and maybe it means working the four-to-closing shift at a burger place with a smile on your face when you don't feel like it. There's holiness in both.

If it sounds as though I'm in favor of your considering only "usual" careers and lifestyles, that's not the case. Lord knows we need priests and sisters and monks, full-time missionaries, and church leaders of all kinds. Too many people who probably *are* called to those vocations don't answer because they're afraid of missing out on happiness. False fear: if you *are* called to that life, you have a head start on happiness because God doesn't call someone to misery.

Point is, real holiness is "available," so to speak, wherever you are unless you're running a drug operation, working as a hit person for the mob, or something like that. It's not something you have to go to an Asian mountaintop to find. It's something you find in yourself and in the circumstances of your life. If you're a student-council rep, going to meetings and trying to make things happen is part of your holiness. If you're an outside linebacker, stopping the ball carrier on a sweep is part of your holiness. If you're living with an alcoholic parent, learning to cope is part of your holiness. And if you're anywhere between puberty and retirement (or maybe even death), learning how to deal correctly with sexuality is *really* part of your holiness.

Going to an Asian mountaintop would be cool, but you won't *find* holiness *there*. The mountaintop will simply provide a spectacular atmosphere and help create a great mood for looking into yourself and discovering your own path to holiness.

Follow it. Maybe it'll take you to far away places and a semi-exotic lifestyle. Maybe it'll take you to Wendy's.

God hangs out everywhere, remember.

Especially inside you.

Paul kept referring to "the holy ones" when he wrote his letters to Christian communities (read 2 Corinthians 13:12; Ephesians 1:1; Philippians 1:1; Colossians 1:2).

Who were those people? Just ordinary Christians, hanging in and trying to do the right thing. Hanging in, making mistakes, asking forgiveness, starting over, hanging in.

People like Francis of Assisi, Joan of Arc, and many other official saints made the holiness headlines. They were terrific, no doubt about it, and we ought to learn from them.

But you're a member of the same club.

CHAPTER THIRTY

· · · · · · · · · · ·

Some Final Stuff

"**A**nd they lived happily ever after."

That really IS supposed to be the ending of everyone's story. Sure would be nice if everyone's story did end that way. Maybe we could arrange it. Might be a good idea to check with the Author.

"This I was trained for," Alexander said quietly as he brought the huge sixteen-wheeler back down to seventy miles per hour. A half mile behind them on Route 47, the black Lincoln exploded several more times and burned even more merrily.

He looked over at Samantha. She had never been more beautiful. Her translucent skin nearly shimmered in the cab of the semi. Her soft red lips were slightly parted. He leaned toward her. She leaned toward him. Ever closer they came. The air between them in the truck turned electric at the approach of their kiss.

Suddenly, they heard the unmistakable whirring above them. Alexander leaned out the window of the cab and looked up at the helicopter filled with a second supply of organized-crime hit men. A machine-gun volley whizzed past his ear.

"Looks like I'll have to take a rain check, sweetheart," Alexander said with a little smile. "Don't worry; this won't take long."

Samantha…

Reader: Excuse me, can I go get a Rolaids?

Author: Just thought we'd do another love scene and car chase before the book ends. I'm getting to like writing them.

Reader: Keep your day job.

Author: Right. Well, this is it. The book's about over. If somebody *made* you read it, as you suggested might be the case (back in chapter 1), I hope you're not holding that against them.

Reader: I won't. I guess you want to know what I think of the book.

Author: That's always on a writer's mind, but it's difficult to find out truthfully, so I seldom ask.

Reader: What do *you* think of it now that it's done?

Author: Great love scenes and car chases.

Reader: No, really.

Author: It left a lot of things out. But then, any book about life and God and all that stuff is going to leave a lot of things out unless you write a library. But maybe that leaves it open to a sequel. In the sequel, Alexander and Samantha...

Reader: Tragically drive off a cliff in the first chapter and are never heard from again. Any final golden thoughts?

Author: Dunno about "golden," but I've got some thoughts. Here's a couple: You're important, and you're wonderful. Now I know that sounds like something you heard in a fourth-grade self-esteem program, but it happens to be true.

Reader: How can you say that when you don't know me, never met me?

Author: Don't have to. Are you breathing?

Reader: Yeah, I developed the habit a long time ago and can't break it.

Author: Bingo. That's all it takes. If you're breathing, you're *here,* and you're here because God decided to put you here, and God doesn't *have* to do anything—that's one of the perks of being God—and God doesn't do anything substandard. God doesn't serve stale bologna. Nothing but prime rib or whatever your favorite comparison might be in God's restaurant. It's hard to believe because, well, as we talked about before, there are so many people that they start to seem ordinary, and it's easy to feel ordinary about yourself. And because we don't always live up to what we are. But that doesn't *change* what we are.

Reader: Anything else?

Author: Life is finding out what's real and what's fake; what's important and what's not; what's true and what's a lie. It's a tricky business because what's fake can look real sometimes, and what doesn't really make any difference can look important for a while, and lies…well, lies can look pretty convincing and attractive. Just check out the snake story back in Genesis, chapter 3.

Reader: So how do you tell the difference?

Author: Keep checking in with God. If there's an easier way, I don't know about it. You just keep checking in with God and asking for direction and listening. I'm convinced that if you keep regularly and honestly—that's a very big word, by the way—checking in with God, you're just not going to get spiritually screwed up all that bad. There's probably a more theological way of putting that idea, but I don't write theology.

I write short notes now and then, though, to people who have been in my classroom. I wrote one once to a past student who was going through some tough times, and it was just "Hang in; we can't afford to lose you. Love, Jim."

I don't know if you're going through tough times right now, but the message pretty well works for all times; and you can remember it if tough times come.

About the Author

In his own words, Jim Auer is "really *old*...I mean, I've been around for *over half a century*." But he remembers what it was like to be a teenager, including the problems and difficulties. "Taking World Culture notes on those stone tablets over the roar of the stupid dinosaurs—now THERE was a drag." He believes in a strongly serious approach to life: "Take my classes, for example—serious, intense stuff, with absolutely no clowning around ever, except on weekdays."

There *is* a serious side to him. He has taught English and religion for over twenty-five years, written eleven books for teens and young adults, and been a friend to three thousand students. Over those years, "I've learned a few things...I'd like to talk about them." In this book, he does. Christian living for today's young person: everything from prayer to sex—straight, no fluff, no lecture, no bull, but with generous helpings of humor.

Jim and his wife of twenty-seven years ("There are definite signs this is the real thing") have a grown son and daughter.